Background

Dear Earl Hipp,

I just want to thank you for writing this book. This world is a very hard place for teenagers to live in. Since I lost my grandmother, I have had two other friends who died. I have been confronted with suicide on more than one occasion, and another friend of mine was shot last year. I live in a nice community, a fairly safe one, but no place is truly untouched by death and violence. It often seems like adults who haven't been confronted with a friend who has thought about or attempted suicide, seen the violence in our world, or felt our grief don't even realize that we grieve. People tend to think we're young and resilient, but they haven't seen the ones who can't deal with the grief. It's nice to know that maybe someone wants to know about our grief. Thank you, God bless.

Mackenzie, Seventeen

Acknowledgments

Thanks to you for having the courage to pick up this book. We live in a culture that is in denial about the complicated emotions surrounding loss and grief. Most people just avoid the topic entirely and stumble through their losses as best they can. This means young people don't have informed guides. Your understanding of this material should make a positive difference in your life and in the lives of people around you.

Thanks to all the young people who shared their stories of loss and grief. Because they shared their experiences, others will learn and feel less alone. It's when we share from the heart that we discover we are much more alike than we are different. We discover that all people, regardless of what they look like on the outside, have common human needs and feelings. Our pains and our joys unite us when we share our stories.

Thanks to the adults working with groups of young people. Many of them helped to get young people's contributions for this book. In their groups, these special people create safe and nurturing environments for young people. In this way they help young people develop the full spectrum of life skills necessary for resilience and strong self-esteem. If you know people doing this work, thank them. They deserve all of our recognition and support.

Thanks to my editors at Hazelden for their continued confidence in me and their caring support at each stage in the creation of this book. It is important to remember that organizations are really made up of people. All of the people I have worked with at Hazelden have expressed a commitment to fostering informed and capable young people.

GETTING THROUGH LOSS

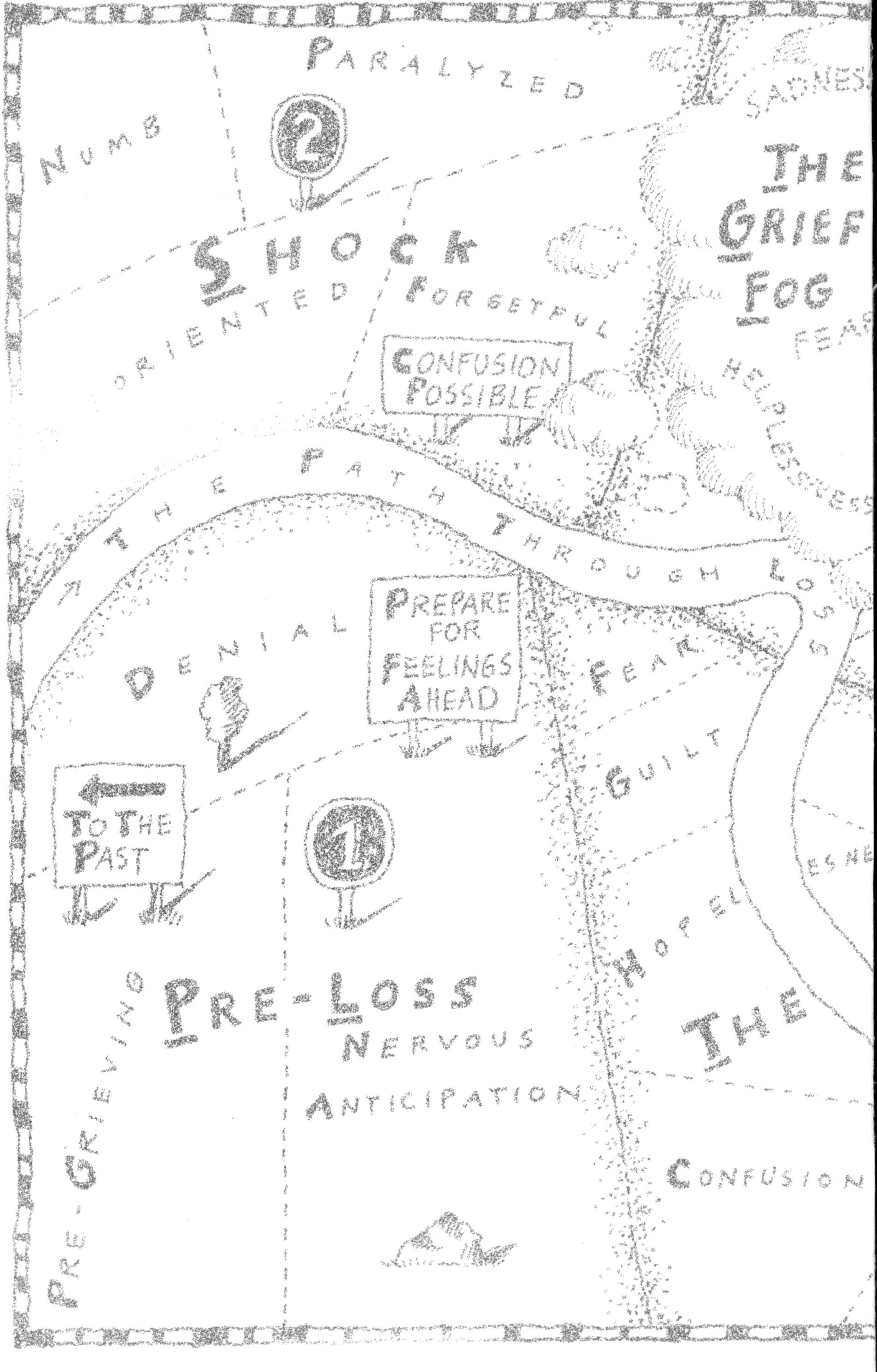

PARALYZED

NUMB

②

SADNESS

SHOCK

THE GRIEF FOG

ORIENTED · FORGETFUL

FEAR

HELPLESSNESS

CONFUSION POSSIBLE

THE PATH THROUGH LOSS

DENIAL

PREPARE FOR FEELINGS AHEAD

FEAR

GUILT

TO THE PAST

①

HOPELESSNESS

PRE-GRIEVING

PRE-LOSS

NERVOUS

ANTICIPATION

THE

CONFUSION

HELP FOR THE HARD TIMES

GETTING THROUGH LOSS

by
Earl Hipp

Illustrations by
L. K. Hanson

Hazelden
Publishing

Hazelden

Center City, Minnesota 55012-0176

ISBN-13: 978-1-56838-085-8
ISBN-10: 1-56838-085-2

Working with them toward that common goal has made a challenging task easier.

Thanks to LK, my partner in this project. Through his graphic arts talent, he makes a difficult subject more understandable and easier to absorb. He is a wonderful person and a gift in my life.

Thanks to my circle of supportive friends. In the joys and struggles of my life they tolerate my weird moments and let me know I'm loved. Pretty nice, don't you think?

Finally, I want to express my gratitude for the spiritual force working in and through my life for making it all possible.

Earl Hipp
Spring 1995

CONTENTS

WHERE TO GO IF:

YOU ARE REALLY HURTING FROM A LOSS

SEVEN THINGS A GRIEVING PERSON NEEDS TO KNOW

HOW TO GET THROUGH A BIG LOSS

SKILLS FOR THE HARD TIMES

YOU WANT TO LEARN ABOUT LOSS AND GRIEF

YOU ARE DEALING WITH OLD LOSSES

EXPLORING YOUR LOSS POT

YOU HAVE A FRIEND IN GRIEF

HOW TO SUPPORT A GRIEVING PERSON

YOU WANT TO KNOW WHAT OTHER YOUNG PEOPLE EXPERIENCED

WHAT KIDS HAVE LEARNED ABOUT LOSS AND GRIEF

INTRODUCTION

This book is a beginning—a book about loss for people who don't know much about this complicated and very personal experience. Because loss is such a big part of everyone's life, it's important to learn about the process of getting through loss. It's important to understand the normal feelings, thoughts, and behaviors associated with grief and to know how to take care of yourself in the healing process. Knowing what to expect makes the experience less scary and increases the likelihood of getting through loss without unnecessary pain.

But there is a problem with books about loss. You read a book using your head, your mind, but you experience loss with your heart. At the center of it all, loss is about feelings, complicated feelings. This book, any book, can be only a guide, a map to help you find your way through difficult emotional territory.

Losses hurt. Big losses hurt more than smaller losses, but they all hurt. I like to think of a big loss as a wound, like a cut. It can be deep and painful, and it can heal cleanly or leave a giant scar. Just as the body works miracles of healing on itself, the heart also naturally knows how to heal from the pain of a loss. The hard part is trusting the healing process. We can't help but have losses; they are part of a normal life. But we can learn how to take care of ourselves so the wound heals cleanly.

It is also important not to focus on just the big losses. As important as they are, they may not account for the majority of losses that we go through in a lifetime. It's the many little losses we experience day after day, year after year, that add up. Thousands of small hurts can collect in a heart and create a growing wound. A lot of small losses can also create a deeply wounded person.

Loss is about contradictions. One of the most important discoveries I hope you'll make is that this is actually a book about gifts. If you know how to find them, if you know how to get through loss and grief in healthy ways, you will receive the gifts of maturity, emotional growth, self-acceptance, connection to others, and more.

My hope is that this book will help you understand what all losses have in common and that you'll learn how to grow through the predictable stages of the grief that follow. I also hope this book will decrease the chances you'll be damaged by a loss and increase the chances you will find the gifts. On the pages that follow, you will find explanations and a map of this complicated emotional territory. Along the way you will hear from lots of young people who have had losses and gotten through. What you will find in the following pages is a caring guide to help you through a current loss or losses to come.

Remember that lots of people gave unselfishly of themselves so this book could be in your hands at this moment. It is the wish of each and every one of them that you feel less alone with your loss. They wanted you to have *Help for The Hard Times*, support for getting through loss.

WHAT IS A LOSS?

LOSS IS AN EVENT

You can think of loss as any event that changes the way things have been. All changes begin with an ending of the way it was. Endings mean separation, missing something that was there before, going on without, no longer having something you loved, letting go. In someway, the world you had gotten used to is suddenly and often dramatically different. The loss is an event, the line in the sand, the moment after which things are different. In large or small ways this moment changes you and your life, sometimes forever.

When people talk about losses they're most often referring to the big, sad losses like a death, the split up of a family, or a long-distance move. But it's also important to know that someone may not have experienced a big loss and can still be profoundly hurt by not knowing how to cope with a lot of smaller losses.

I was eight years old when I had my first big loss. My grandmother (who I was very close to) died of cancer. A lot of people assumed that as an eight-year-old I couldn't really understand or that if I acted okay I was. Eight-year-olds understand death, what it means, and feel emotions at least as intense as any adult. Only they don't know the ways to express all that they're feeling. My grandmother's death completely shattered the security of my world.
—Mackenzie, Seventeen

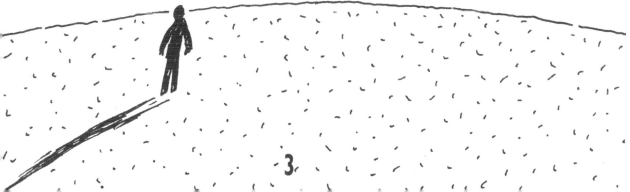

Sometimes the good things in life can also
bring losses. For example, you might have a
new baby in your family but lose the privacy of
your own room. Your family might get a new
house, but you may lose your friends in the old
neighborhood. Perhaps you get to go to a new
school as you get older, but you lose your
status as the older kid and become a beginner
again. In each of these cases something that
people consider positive happens, but the
result is that you have to give up how it was,
deal with your complicated feelings, and figure
out how to go on.

Another kind of loss that can add up over
time is *future loss*. Future loss happens when you don't get something you expected. Examples of a future loss might include

- **Not getting a promised gift**
- **Having a date cancel**
- **No longer feeling safe in your home, school, or neighbor-hood**
- **Not making the team**
- **Not graduating**
- **Becoming disabled**
- **Not going on a trip that you were looking forward to**

In these examples you lose the future you were expecting.
Sometimes a future loss results in something positive happening,
but that doesn't always lessen the pain of the loss.

Then there are the thousands of little losses that happen all the
time. Having brothers or sisters get things you don't, losing your homework assignment, finding your favorite clothing damaged, missing the
bus, being threatened in school, adults lying to you, friendships ending, losing your house keys—all are examples of smaller losses that
happen regularly. But in every case, something is gone or ended, you
have feelings about it, and you have to go on with your life.

Some losses are obviously more important than others because
they result in bigger changes in our lives. The loss of your house
keys is obviously not as threatening as the death of a family member, for example. But with every loss, regardless how big, your life is

changed—sometimes in little ways that you get over quickly and sometimes in big ways that change you and your life forever.

We can never go back again, that much is certain.

—Daphne du Maurier

Loss is the *event* that changes how things were; it's the ending. The loss sets off lots of complicated feelings and leaves us with the problem of how to keep on living from then on. We'll talk more about those challenges later,

I had expected to make the sixth grade traveling basketball team because I had been on the team in fifth grade, but I didn't. I felt ashamed and unhappy, because I love to play. As a result of not making the team though, I got to be in a spring musical at my church, so it turned out to be good I guess.

—Rachel, Fourteen

but for the moment it's enough to learn to recognize and name loss events. If you're not aware you are experiencing a loss, you risk adding to the hurt, burying your feelings, and carrying your sadness around... forever.

If you are aware that you are going through a loss, you can decide what you want to do about it. As you learn helpful ways to grow through the losses in your life, you can take better care of yourself and find more of the gifts that are available. Step one, then, is to learn more about this complicated human experience called loss.

Understanding Loss

To build an understanding of loss, let's take a closer look at some of the different types of losses you might have in your life.

There are two ways to talk about losses. The first way is to describe the many different *kinds* of loss events, things that can happen that create a loss for us. The second way is to talk about the *intensity* of a loss, the impact a specific loss has on your life. Let's begin by exploring the enormous variety of loss events that can occur in a person's life.

KINDS OF LOSSES

Kinds of Losses

It is impossible to list all of the kinds of loss events because there are so many. The following list gives some examples of losses that young people say they've experienced. As you go through the list, see if you can tell *what is being lost* as a result of each event.

PARENTS DIVORCING

LOSING A LIBRARY BOOK

NOT GETTING THE CLASS, TEACHER OR SCHOOL YOU WANTED

BEING PUT IN ADVANCED CLASSES, LEAVING FRIENDS BEHIND

REALIZING THERE IS NO SANTA

BREAKING UP WITH A GIRLFRI...

NEW BABY IN THE FAMILY

TEAM JACKET GETS STOLEN

NOT MAKING THE TEAM

GETTING A JOB

DEATH OF A FRIEND

GRADUATING

PHYSICAL ABUSE

LOSING WEIGHT

MOVING TO A NEW SCHOOL

GOING TO A NEW FOSTER HOME

FAILING A TEST

LOSING A FAVORITE OBJECT

BEING PICKED ON AT SCHOOL

BEING PUT DOWN BY A PARENT

You can probably think of a many more examples because there are so many ways to experience a loss. It's important to remember that all changes, even the good ones, begin with an ending. When good things happen, the way life used to be is gone... and that is about loss.

When I was twelve or thirteen years old my dog died. I grew up with that dog. I cried forever and really hated the new dog we got. After my dog died, I was mad at everything. I was really insecure about stuff. I can't remember how long it took to feel normal, but I learned to like our new dog. I never forgot, but I took the medicine. I felt bad that I hated the new dog.

—Joshua, Seventeen

Intensity of Loss

Another way to think about a loss event is by considering its intensity, its strength. The intensity of a loss is directly related to its impact on your life. The size of the changes in your daily life, the power of the feelings that result, and the difficulty of adjusting to life after the loss—all are measures of how intense we feel about a given loss event.

It is important to know that everyone copes with loss differently. It's not uncommon for one person to be wiped out by a loss, while another person may be totally unaffected by the same event. So when we describe the intensity of a loss, we have to leave a lot of room for individual differences. What's most important is how intense the loss is *for you*. You are entitled to your feelings regardless of what people around you feel or think. With that in mind, let's look at three general intensity categories.

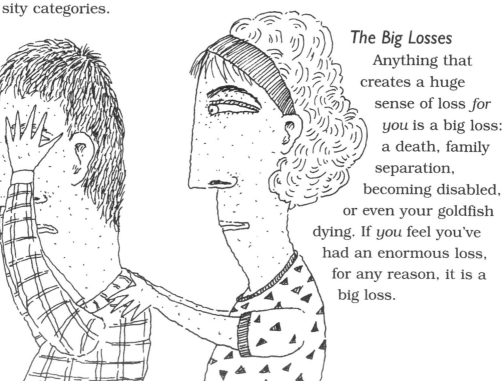

The Big Losses

Anything that creates a huge sense of loss *for you* is a big loss: a death, family separation, becoming disabled, or even your goldfish dying. If *you* feel you've had an enormous loss, for any reason, it is a big loss.

The Not-So-Big Losses

Any experience that is hard, sad, or very difficult for you to accept is a not-so-big loss. These losses are not as earth-shaking as a big loss, but they are still important and a big challenge to get through. Something like changing schools, a friend moving away, a relationship ending, or anything difficult for *you* to handle can be a not-so-big loss.

The Small Losses

Losses that are frustrating, annoying, or disappointing for you are small losses. They might include not getting a class or teacher you wanted, being disappointed by a friend, losing a homework assignment, your brother or sister getting something you didn't, and so on.

Losses affect different people in different ways. The reasons for these differences don't matter. We are all put together differently, and it's important to respect each other's responses to a loss. There is no "right" way to go through a loss. Be very patient with yourself and others who are experiencing losses. *Never, never* put yourself down for not having an "appropriate" reaction or for not reacting like someone else. As you will learn, loss is a very complicated and deeply personal experience. Whatever your response looks like, it is okay. It's you being you.

> I lost my best friend when I was fourteen, not cause she died, but because I was heavy into drugs. She tried to help me by telling my mom. I got so mad I told her if I ever saw her again I'd kill her. Down the line I realized my drug problem. I had drowned myself into pot so heavily I could not remember reality. I had a long and hard struggle to quit. After that, I realized that she had cared so much about my drug problem she risked our friendship to help me. I regret what I said to her. I lost a real friend.
>
> —Bridget, Fifteen

> I got robbed. I got back to normal on pay day; then I wasn't broke. Now I don't carry all my money with me. I learned to keep a grip on my ends.
>
> —Tony, Fifteen

A Personal Loss History

Now that you have an understanding of the types of events that can be considered a loss, and a way to think about the intensity of any single loss event (big, not-so-big, and small), you can look at the history of loss in your life. This will help you to get a big picture of the number, types, and intensity of the losses in your life.

Draw a long line on a blank piece of paper. Put zero on the left end and your current age on the right. Divide your age by two and put that number in the middle. This is your life line.

LIFE LINE

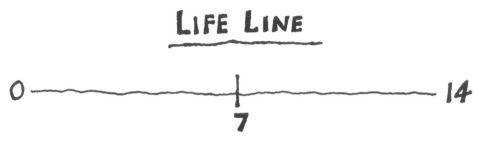

Look at the list of loss events and see how many of them you have experienced in your life. Add any others unique to your life that are not on the list. Put a *B* alongside those that were really intense, an *NSB* for those that were important but not major life changers, and an *S* by the smaller losses. You can actually plot them out on your life line to see a picture of the different periods in your life.

BECKY'S LIFE LINE

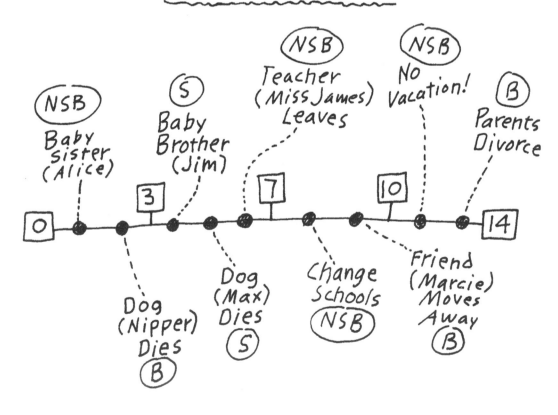

With each loss event on your list, try to remember what ended, what you had to go on without, and what feelings you had. As you go through the book you will learn to better understand and cope with all the losses in your life. You can then return to your life line and consider how well you handled your losses and if they had any lasting effects on you.

Our greatest glory consists not in never falling, but in rising every time we fall.

—Ralph Waldo Emerson

In Becky's life line, only a few of the losses she experienced would fit. As she did this activity she discovered that there were really lots of losses in her life and that she still felt sad about some of them. What we learn from this exercise is that even a young person has somehow managed to get through a lot of losses. Our next step then is to learn *how* we got through our losses. What skills have we been using to get through loss, for better or worse?

Unlearning and Relearning Lessons about Loss

As you can see, just living means experiencing loss. It also means that we've somehow learned to cope with big, not-so-big, and small losses and have been doing so since we were little kids. Just because we've been coping with loss doesn't mean we have been getting through it as well as we can. No one teaches us how to get through all the complicated feelings and problems that come with loss. Think about it: where did you learn how to get through a big loss?

Most people learn how to handle losses by watching adults (who also didn't get training), movies, and television. Given the number of people that die in movies and on TV, we really don't see many people grieving.

Most of us learned the most powerful lessons about handling loss early in our lives from the adults around us. As you watched them react to their losses, you learned their way of coping with feelings. For better or worse, many of us are still using the lessons we learned as little children to deal with the losses we face today.

Go back to your life line and choose one of your losses. For that loss, see if you can remember what the adults in your world taught you about how to behave when going through a loss. What did they say or do that suggested what you should feel or how you should behave?

What Did Your Parents Teach You about Coping with a Loss?

Well, my parents never told me anything about how you feel when you lose someone, so I've never told people in the past how I felt. I just went out and took it out on people. I didn't even know what I was doing. But I can't really blame that on my parents because my dad's been through a lot with Vietnam and everything in his past. So I really don't tell him much about how I feel or what's going on in my life. Well, my mom, she can't even help herself when her own cat dies, so how's she going to help me?

—Shawnee, Seventeen

Parents know nothing about loss or how to treat their children. They seem to think that you need to get on with things RIGHT AWAY, instead of letting us figure out what the deal is.

—Megan, Sixteen

I've never had a big loss in my life, but someone I know was killed in a drive-by on the west side of Chicago. My mother didn't concern herself with it, so neither did I, so it didn't matter. There was no love lost when the event happened because that's how I was taught to care about things. I didn't show any feelings cause as long as it's not important to my mom, it doesn't matter.

—Sita, Fourteen

We talked about death as a family. It helped.

—Chad, Sixteen

When I was five my stepgrandfather died. I always had thought of him as my real grandfather. My parents would not let me go to the funeral. I didn't understand that. I realize that I didn't know what to do at a funeral but it would have helped to be able to say good-bye in my own way. I guess the lessons I got were, don't handle it with much emotion, don't talk about it, and handle it by yourself.

—Vanessa, Eighteen

When I was little, my mom comforted me after a loss and told me about each stage of life and that people have their natural journey of life.

—Steven, Nineteen

Women cry and men look sad.

—Heidi, Fifteen

Crying is okay.

—Mike, Nineteen

If loss and living go hand in hand, you need to have the best skills possible. You will want to know how to steer your way through losses with the least damage and as much growth as possible. Because the skills for growing through loss are not taught anywhere, most people will have to start over. This may mean unlearning some of the lessons you got that are not helpful and relearning better responses.

> ## *Surviving meant being born over and over.*
>
> *—Erica Jong*

The basic lessons for learning to cope with loss in helpful ways include

- Learning to *understand the complicated feelings* that accompany all losses
- Learning how to *get through the grief and pain* of our losses
- Learning what to do to *take care of ourselves* while we are healing

WHAT IS GRIEF?
GRIEF IS A COMPLICATED EMOTIONAL EXPERIENCE

Because all losses evoke similar feelings, a good place to begin developing our loss skills is with learning to understand the very personal and complicated world of feelings we call "grief."

Loss is what happens, *grief* is how people feel as a result. Sometimes grief is powerful and complicated, other times it is not at all hard to get through. But all losses, even the little ones, generate feelings. The bigger the loss, the more complicated the feelings. Let's take a closer look at all the feelings we could include when we use the word "grief."

IT'S PERFECTLY *NORMAL* TO HAVE SOME OR ALL OF THE FOLLOWING FEELINGS WHEN EXPERIENCING LOSS:
Sadness, confusion, anger, hopelessness, fear, loneliness, crabbiness, relief, wild laughter, embarrassment, fatigue, guilt, worry, disappointment, helplessness, resentment, and low self-esteem... just for starters.

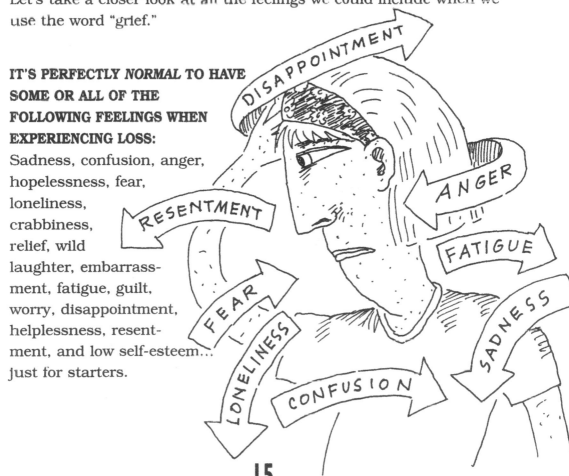

> ### *Experience is a good teacher, but she sends in terrific bills.*
>
> —*Minna Antrim*

Each feeling can be so intense it knocks you down or so subtle you barely notice. The feelings also seem to *come and go at different times.* After a big loss, you can be laughing at one moment and a second later be really angry or find yourself in tears as a memory floats by. You can feel mild frustration or blow up in an angry tantrum at the slightest little thing.

Grief is many different feelings going on in you *at the same moment.* That is why a grieving person can be crying about something sad and at the same time be laughing at how crazy it all seems. It is why you can be really angry at someone and feel love for the person at the same time. The emotions are all there and cooking away, but the one that is on top is the one that gets most of our attention.

Grieving is like watching a merry-go-round. One minute you are looking at the white horse, and a second later it's gone and you're

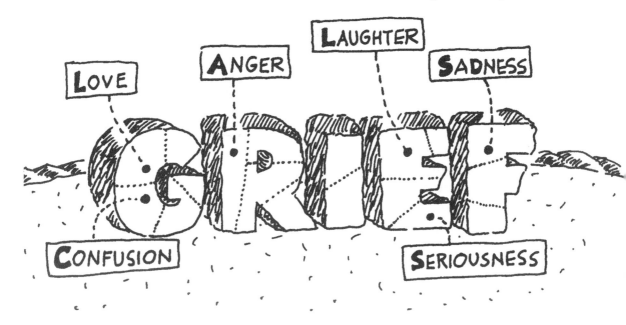

watching the red horse, and then the blue horse. They all keep coming past and asking for your attention. Part of the reason grief is so complicated is that you have so many feelings that change so quickly. Right after a big loss, the merry-go-round of feelings is spinning so fast, you can hardly see any horse.

Another important thing to know is that all of these feelings can be going on inside you whether or not you are aware of them. Consider the ocean's undertow. The surface of the ocean might look calm, but at the shore there can be powerful below-the-surface currents that can pull a swimmer out into the deep water. In the same way, if you aren't aware of the feelings of loss, you can think you're okay but not be aware that you are becoming a more sad, serious, and angry person.

Because each person's emotional experience of loss is different and very complex, it's difficult to explain. So we simply use the word "grief" as a shorthand description. The danger of using that description is that we are tempted to think of grief as one feeling instead of a tangled mix of complicated and sometimes contradictory emotions.

YOU
CAN'T STOP
GRIEF!

Grief Happens

Grief happens. Period. Whether you know it, like it, want it, need it, feel like it, enjoy it, or appreciate it— whether you are ready for it or not—the feelings associated with loss just happen in you because you are a normal human being.

Because we've all learned different ways to deal with loss, we may not always be aware of the emotions going on inside us. But whether or not you express your feelings, you will experience grief after a loss. You can ignore your feelings or even find ways to run from them. But the grief still happens. The right question is not, "*Should* I grieve this loss?" but, "*How open am I to experiencing* the feelings about this loss that are going on in me right now?"

Later we'll discuss some of the things you can do to have a healthy, self-loving, and positive response to a loss. You will learn how you can take care of yourself in the grieving and healing process. These skills are not about avoiding grief but how to get through it with minimum damage and find some of the gifts along the way. It's important to remember that no matter what you do, you can't stop grief. It just happens.

Grief Depends on Who You Are

The intensity of a loss, how powerful a given loss is for you, depends on who you are. What can be a devastating loss for one person can be easy for another. How people handle a loss depends on how they are put together. It depends on what they learned about handling loss from their cultural background and from their families. The number of losses they have experienced, their age, and how much support they have all contribute to how well people will handle a loss. It is a very individual thing. Let's see how these factors can help with loss.

Cultural Differences

It is important to recognize that different cultures treat loss and grief in very different ways. When looking at someone else's beliefs and rituals around loss, you have to remember that you are looking through your own ideas about what is "normal" or "appropriate."

For example, this book looks at loss primarily from a North American perspective. Other cultures and spiritual traditions view loss and grief differently.

- On one island in the South Pacific, people who are unconscious are considered dead. Because of this belief, in this culture people are able to "die" a number of times.

- In some parts of Brazil, people are very poor and many children die quite young. In this culture people believe that most infant and child deaths are a direct result of the child's will to live. They feel that if a child dies, then apparently, he or she just didn't want to live. For this reason children are typically not mourned for more than a few days.

- In Bali, people believe the gods will not listen to your prayers if you're not calm. So grieving people there are very careful to be in control of their feelings. Heavy grieving is thought to be a threat to health and makes you a target for evil spirits.

- The Ifaluk, people from a small island in the Pacific Ocean, believe that after a really good cry they will forget the person who died and get back to feeling normal. Someone who keeps on grieving in their culture is considered not mentally healthy.

Native Americans have dance, ceremonies, and are very religious. That helped me a lot when my sister was killed. I want to learn more. I don't know enough about my Native American culture.

—Sean, Thirteen

I am a Buddhist. We put fruits up on a shelf to honor the deceased. Sometimes we have special days to pray for them, but they are always honored in special ways.

—Vantram, Fourteen

In the Jewish tradition we have Shiva. For seven days after a death, lots of friends and relatives visit the grieving person to listen, cry, laugh, tell stories, feed them, or just sit and be quiet.

—Judith, Eighteen

• In China, grief is expressed through physical problems or by arguing with others. Letting people know that you are not feeling well or that you are having a hard time getting along with others is how you show everyone you are grieving.

Even if these ideas seem strange to you, they are normal for the people living in these cultures. That's why it's so important to accept that each person grieves in his or her own way. We must be sensitive to and tolerant of whatever someone does to get through the very human experiences of loss and grief.

Your own cultural heritage may offer methods you can use to help you through your grief process. It doesn't matter if you deal with your losses differently from others around you. **The only important consideration is, Does your way of grieving help *you* deal with loss?**

Different Families Have Different Skills

Just as different cultures have different ways of dealing with grief, every family handles loss in its own way. Your family does too, whether you are aware of it or not. You can tell what the rules are by noticing how people relate to each other during a loss—what they talk or don't talk about, whether or not people express their feelings, and how they support each other as they go through their grieving. Sometimes it's easier to see the rules in someone else's family than in yours. The lessons you learned in your own family may be harder to see because they have always been a normal part of your life.

Some families are better at handling loss than others. A young person experiencing loss would be very fortunate to be with adults who

- **Can always be supportive and comforting**

- **Have the time and patience to be there for you while you express your feelings**

- **Encourage you to participate in family activities that help resolve grief**

- **Listen and listen and listen until you are done talking about how mad, sad, fearful, confused, or frustrated you feel, even if it takes months... or years**

20

This kind of family environment promotes healing for everyone. Unfortunately, it's an unusual family that can operate in this way.

On the other hand, a family can experience a huge loss and not show any feelings, hardly mention it to anyone, and not talk about it in family life. Family members may go about life as if nothing ever happened and even get angry if you bring up the subject. It can be very difficult to heal cleanly from your losses if you come from a family that doesn't know how to deal with grief.

For most of us, the reality is somewhere in the middle. Depending on the importance of the loss, family members may be able to be there for you some of the time, with some of what you need, but probably not for as long as you need it. With a big loss, even the most loving parents, brothers, sisters, or other relatives may have such a hard time with their own grief that they can't help you much at all.

Number of Losses

Some people have had lots and lots of loss in their life. In a way, they get used to it. That doesn't mean they don't feel hurt, sad, or angry. It's just that they aren't as surprised by loss when it comes along. They have adapted and for them it's just "another" loss. However, just because a person appears to be handling loss is no guarantee that he or she doesn't hurt deep inside. What's showing on the outside doesn't always tell you much about the wound that may be growing on the inside.

A good example of this is what happens during a war. In situations where people witness a lot of death, lose friends, and live in fear for their lives day after day, they have to put their feelings away in order to survive. In a sense, they have adapted to loss as a "normal" part of life in order to keep

21

going. This can also happen in communities where violence and guns and people getting killed are a "normal" part of community life. Sometimes it is not until years later, when people are living very different lives, that they can let down their guard. Then the old stuffed feelings begin to leak through and cause fears, nightmares, confusion, and sometimes angry, aggressive behavior. This is called post-traumatic stress disorder.

People who have lots and lots of loss in their lives and who don't know how to grow through it are setting themselves up for big problems later in life. They will also have problems dealing with future losses. That's why it's important to learn to get through each loss when it occurs.

Age

Being older helps. Plain old experience with living teaches us that even the biggest losses are survivable. Unfortunately, we have to learn that lesson from experience, and that means going through the grieving process... again and again. It's not fun but it does change our perspective. We learn we will make it through a loss.

> *Life has got to be lived— that's all there is to it. At seventy I would say the advantage is that you take life more calmly. You know that, "This too, shall pass!"*
>
> —*Eleanor Roosevelt*

Every age has its own kinds of losses. A very young person may feel she can't survive the death of her first goldfish. In that moment, for that little person, the world looks like it is going to end and no amount of explaining will help. Having a best friend move away may be more survivable at eighteen than at ten. The ending of a romantic relationship may be a little easier at twenty-five than sixteen, and so on.

As we get older and live through more and more losses, we learn that we can survive the pain of a loss. But at each age we have to learn these lessons again for a new set of losses. Experience helps. Being older doesn't relieve us from having losses or from the sadness of grieving, but it does help.

> *... suffering... no matter how multiplied, is always individual.*
>
> —Anne Morrow Lindbergh

Two years ago, two boys from our school were killed in a car accident. One of the boys was dating my close friend. They had been testing a car on a winding road and struck a tree at close to 90 mph. This devastated the community. It put a lot into perspective and reminded me again that just because I'm young does not mean I am invincible.

—Summer, Seventeen

Supports

Grieving alone is terrible. When everything feels like darkness and there is no one to remind you of the light, your grief is deepened. When you feel like no one understands or cares and there is no one around to prove you wrong, you invite depression and hopelessness.

In the moments when we are lost in feelings of grief, getting support can be very important. Our grief is ours alone. But without caring, understanding, encouragement, compassion, and the objectivity of others, we will likely be more deeply wounded by our losses.

> *Shared joy is double joy, and shared sorrow is half-sorrow.*
>
> —Swedish proverb

People with caring and available family members, a strong circle of friends, or good community connections are in a better position not to suffer alone. As a result, they are less likely to be self-destructive and more likely to heal cleanly.

Learning to Recognize Grief

It may sound strange, but people who are very aware of the feelings associated with grief are lucky. When you are aware that you have experienced a loss (of any intensity) you then have the opportunity to consciously choose your response. You can make the positive choices to take care of yourself during your healing process. By consciously making positive choices, you are more likely to actually grow through your loss instead of being wounded by the experience.

The problem is that most of us haven't had much training about grief and loss. Without awareness and understanding of what we are experiencing, small losses and even some big losses can pass through our lives relatively unnoticed. We keep the feelings inside, hidden, underground, unconscious. If the world on the outside ignores our losses, we may also try to "just get over it." Driving grief deep inside is never a good idea, but if we don't understand the experience, if we don't know how to take care of ourselves, we have almost no choice.

Many young people will have to start from scratch to learn how to recognize when they have had a loss and when they are grieving.

Signals a Person Is Grieving

To help you become better able to recognize grief, consider the following list of symptoms common to grieving people. The signals that a person is grieving vary greatly from person to person, day to day, and by the importance and intensity of a loss. Symptoms can come and go quickly. You can have one, a few, or all of the symptoms in any given moment. See if this list reminds you of anyone you know.

WATCH FOR SIGNALS OF GRIEVING AHEAD

- Feeling embarrassed and unsure

- Making mistakes

- Hopelessness

- Loss of energy, motivation, and optimism

- Being really tired all the time

- Physical problems

- Quick mood changes

- Anger at people, traffic, God, the Universe ...

- Loss of appetite or eating all the time

- Wanting to sleep all the time

- Behaving weirdly or inappropriately

- Inability to think of anything but the loss

- Sadness—sometimes overwhelming

- Losing interest in daily activities

- The "Whys?"—Why me? Why now? Why them? Being obsessed with trying to figure out why things happen the way they do

- Sudden feelings of desperation or hopelessness

- Inability to concentrate

- Wetting the bed

- Nightmares

As difficult as these symptoms sound, they are examples of what a *normal* person might experience when going through loss. Think of loss as a physical, mental, emotional, and spiritual wound. These symptoms are the physical, mental, emotional, and spiritual expression of the pain. If you don't know when you are grieving, you won't know how to take care of yourself.

If you have many of the symptoms on the list, you might be going through a grief experience. There could be other causes, but at the minimum these symptoms indicate that self-care is in order. You may want to reach out for help to understand your feelings and behavior and to get some support. Remember, your experience of grief is normal for you, and that is all that counts, so don't judge yourself. If you reach out for help and understanding, you will learn and grow from your experience.

Why and How People Avoid Grief

My first big loss was my father. No, he didn't die; he moved out. We were very close. I was his "little girl," his "little baby." I was nine when it all began. My parents had many problems and just couldn't get along. I really miss the way we used to be together, and I don't think my family life will ever be normal again. Sure, the pain is mostly gone and I guess in that sense I am normal again, but there is still that thought that comes to mind often, "Why me, why us?"

—Tara, Sixteen

I tried staying away from my Grandparent's house so I wouldn't have to remember all the good times with Grandpa, but I realized that was the wrong decision.

—Becky, Sixteen

Too Big, Too Complicated, Too Scary

Grief is very complicated, scary, and uncomfortable emotional territory. Few of us have the words to explain such a confusing and deeply personal emotional experience. Even if we are able and willing to talk about it, we may not have support people who will hang in there with us while we go through our big feelings. Often, we have to struggle through our losses pretty much alone.

We get exhausted from mood swings and almost always feel tired and used up. We often take side trips into weird thinking or even self-destructive behaviors. What we want more than anything is for life to get back to normal... which it refuses to do.

Friends wonder why you're "not getting over it," and at times you even wonder if there is something wrong with you because you don't seem to be making any progress. Grieving is just hard.

Because grief is obviously not a comfortable, happy, or especially pleasant process, no one looks forward to the experience. In fact, whether they realize it or not, many people try to avoid the discomforts of grieving entirely.

A Thousand Ways to "Go Away"

Avoiding grief doesn't fix things. It only temporarily distracts you from the sadness and discomfort. Some people spend a whole lifetime running from the feelings associated with major losses. But you can't get away from who you are. It is like that old saying "Wherever you go, there you are." When and if you stop running from your grief, it will still be there to deal with, no matter how many years it takes. Sometimes our grief is so overwhelming that we make a conscious decision to just put it away.

Whatever the reason, "going away" from grief is a common choice.

For better or worse, there are a thousand ways people can avoid the difficult grieving process. But remember, they are all temporary.

Denial—Pretending It Didn't Happen

Some people are so unable to deal with their losses that they have to shut down totally. They pretend nothing has happened and that things are like they have always been. They don't want to hear or see anything that refers to the loss, and they work very hard at ignoring the physical and emotional signals associated with grief.

People who are in denial about a loss are very vulnerable. They have to be very threatened by the loss to go to all the effort of holding off the reality. If you come in contact with someone in denial, remember this person is very fragile.

> *When my grandpa died, I was fourteen years old and we knew he was going to die from cancer, but I really didn't realize he was gone till about two months after he died. I just thought of it like he was on vacation and he would be back.*
>
> *—Becky, Sixteen*

After a big loss, everyone has some degree of protective denial. It shields us from the full impact of all the changes the loss will create until we are ready to take them on. Denial can last for a few days or for weeks. In some cases, people never acknowledge the full impact of the loss. The feelings are stuffed, temporarily avoided, but carried around forever.

Masking Feelings with Chemicals

Another way to try to avoid complicated and uncomfortable feelings is to use chemicals to make you less aware. The problem is that the bigger the feelings you are running from, the more of your drug of choice you have to use to escape. It creates a terrible and vicious circle, and eventually you have to sober up or come down and face your life again. When you do, all the stuff you've been running from will be there waiting for you (plus a lot more because using drugs always creates problems).

I lost a girlfriend because I was using drugs. I was really in love (or the closest thing I've ever had) when I ended up taking so many drugs that I lost my head. I began to let drugs be more important than showing my girlfriend that I cared. I ended up losing my relationship with her, and the fact I could not see her anymore was a reality I could not deal with. I began to take more drugs to ease the pain physically and emotionally. I found that facing reality was the only way to finally comprehend that my drugs and my insane life had driven this girl away.

—Brian, Seventeen

Minimizing the Loss

Another way to avoid grief is to pretend it's not as important or as emotionally powerful as it really is. Sometimes parents will put on a tough front when a child's pet dies, in a mistaken attempt to soften the blow for the child or for themselves. A person minimizing a loss might say something like, "It's just a dog," or "She was old and lived a good life," or "Stop crying and pull yourself together." The message is that the loss is not all that important and you shouldn't be so troubled by it. People who minimize a loss are telling you they are in protective denial; they are making a statement about their inability to cope with their own grief feelings.

If you avoid expressing your feelings about a loss, it means those feelings have to go underground. Stuffing feelings is almost never a good choice because we need to experience our grief in order to learn, mature, and grow through our losses. Minimizing and completely denying loss are shields that only *temporarily* let a person avoid the feelings associated with grief.

Masking Feelings with Compulsive Behaviors

People can also get so involved with some small aspect of life that they become too busy to experience their feelings. Some people try to lose themselves in work. Working on something "important" from the moment they get up until late at night and always thinking or worrying about work-related issues is how they go away from their grief feelings.

> *I got the blues thinking of the future,*
> *so I left off and made some marmalade.*
> *It's amazing how it cheers one up*
> *to shred oranges and scrub the floor.*
>
> —D. H. Lawrence

Taking time out from your grief to be in the world, to do some homework, cook a meal, or wash the floor can actually be comforting. But when you *have to* wash all the floors in the house, and do it every day, you are caught up in a vicious circle.

There are lots and lots of other ways to compulsively be involved with some piece of life so you don't have to experience and deal with your feelings. You can constantly listen to music, wearing headphones every moment you're away from a sound system. You can become preoccupied with gambling, video games, television, homework, sleeping, shopping, dating, sports, smoking, or drugs. There are even cases of people who became obsessed with washing their hands every five minutes as a way to stay away from the feelings inside of them.

The problem with compulsive behaviors is that the bigger the feelings, the more of the behavior you have to do to stay ahead of your feelings. Being so preoccupied also creates lots of other problems in your life. Running away from grief feelings is harder than finding your way through them... and when you quit running, they are always there anyway.

Ideally, you will develop the understanding, skills, and supports to be able to face your losses and grow through them. You've already got a great start because you are reading this book. It is important to learn how to confront the feelings that come with loss because otherwise you will find a thousand ways to temporarily stuff those feelings in the loss pot.

WHAT IS THE LOSS POT? A BIG SAD STEW

Some people were never taught how to cope with grief and loss in positive ways. They can't cry easily to release their sadness. Others don't know how, aren't willing, or don't have people to talk to about their sadness, anger, fears, or other feelings. *Whether they realize it or not*, they are keeping a lot of hurt and pain stuffed inside. When people hold back feelings about loss, the feelings get all mixed up inside of them. It is as if all those feelings and hurts go into a big holding tank I call a "loss pot."

You can think of a loss pot as something like a big stew pot. If you're making a stew, you put in a lot of ingredients—meat, potatoes, vegetables, and broth. Then you put a lid on it, put it on the stove, and let it cook. After a while you have a blend that has one common flavor and a few pieces of the original ingredients floating around.

A loss pot is like a stew filled with unpleasant ingredients.

It happened such a long time ago that I can't feel the feelings I should have. I really don't remember much. But I was always told my cousin was cleaning a gun and got shot. Most of all, I guess I'm angry at him and everyone because I didn't find out until I was twelve that he had shot himself in the head.

—Melissa, Fourteen

If you have a lot of losses and you ignore your feelings, you'll have emotions like hurt, confusion, frustration, hopelessness, guilt, and lots of anger all swimming around in your loss pot. Just like in the stew, they get all mixed up and blended together and you wind up with a lot of general sadness. Over time, you add feelings about new losses to the feelings about the old losses. It all gets mixed up and just sits there in the pot slowly cooking away.

Eventually, you don't remember many details of individual losses, just that some sad things happened. All that is left over is this big sad stew.

Carrying all that hurt with you through your life is a lot of work, and it makes you more confused, sad, serious, depressed, or angry than you need to be. Unfortunately, the world is a little crazy when it comes to supporting people in grief. The result is that there are lots of people with full loss pots walking around.

How the World Is Crazy When It Comes to Losses

The world we live in does *not* go out of its way to help people who are grieving. People sometimes behave as though they really don't want to know much about others' issues and feelings. We give each other lots of subtle messages about how to deal with the complicated feelings of grief and how to relate to people with losses. In a way, we live in a world that almost encourages you to keep the lid on your loss pot. These messages are hidden in how we relate to each other and in our customs and beliefs. You have to look really close to find them. Here is a short list. See if any of them sound familiar.

I Don't Want to Hear It

There is a funny custom that goes like this: When someone says, "Hi, how are you doing?" most people just respond with, "Fine, how about you?" Of course it depends

on who is asking, but for the most part, we don't really answer the question. You know they don't really want to know how bad you're feeling. It's as if we have made this pact with each other to pretend everything is okay.

Look Good No Matter What

Because people don't talk much about the really hard stuff in their lives, it is easy to assume (wrongly) that everyone else is having this great life and just handling whatever comes along. Because everyone looks pretty good on the outside, we also want to appear put-together. This is another reason why when someone asks us, "How are you?" we just say, "Fine." In our world it is important to appear put-together, to look good on the outside no matter what you are feeling on the inside.

Handle Problems by Yourself

It is amazing, but when people have big problems, they will often try to deal with them on their own. It is as if we have all learned this silly lesson that if we can't handle it by ourselves, we're weak or incompetent in some way. This is crazy thinking because we're all going to come up against problems we are not equipp handle. In those moments a psychologically healt will recognize that he or she doesn't have the and will instinctively reach out for help a the reality is that people most often s

perately trying with poor tools to make it on their own. The absence of readily available, confidential, emotionally supportive, and helpful people for young people with problems sends a subtle message. It says that young people's problems aren't that important, and if you have problems, you should be able to handle them by yourself.

Be Tough, Play Hard

The superheroes and high-powered police in the movies all seem to get through whatever crisis they are facing with little damage. They can be shot, bleeding, threatened, or beaten up, but somehow they keep going. And no matter how bad a mess they are in, after an hour or two the show will be over and they will be all right. They are tough individuals who see lots of violent death and never cry or grieve their losses. The message we get is to harden up, be tough. If you feel pain, just keep going; you will eventually be okay.

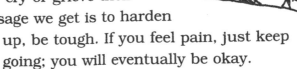

Get Over It Quickly

This is the age of MTV and channel surfing. Things move fast. If we are watching a TV program we don't like, we can push a button and quickly go to a program we like better. We want to do that in our lives too. Because our own loss pots get stirred up around grieving people, *we* get uncomfortable and want them to get over it

quickly. We get impatient with them and give them subtle or not-so-subtle hints that we'd like them to get on with life, get better, feel better... now.

Leave Grieving People Alone

This is the excuse we use to avoid people who are experiencing major grief. Being around grieving people creates reminders of our own similar hurts. It's also difficult to know what to say or how to support a person experiencing a major loss. Because it's complicated and we're uncomfortable, it's easier and simpler just to avoid the grieving person.

It is true that grieving people do need some time alone. But it's also true that even while they are taking their alone time, they need to know people care. They need to know that their friends and family will be there for them when being alone is no longer comfortable. (See "How To Support a Grieving Person," page 101.)

It's No Big Thing

As an attempt to help people experiencing loss, people will sometimes give you a "no big thing" kind of response. Statements like "Just get another (dog, car, friend, school...)," or "Oh, you can handle this," tend to lessen the impact of the event. It's a misguided attempt to support you from someone w'
probably cares
But the _hi'_
"Please don't ha'
this because _I'm_ uncor

Handle It Like an Adult

This is a version of "It's No Big Thing." People do get better at handling losses as they get older and have more experience. That's why it's easy for an adult to forget or not even notice the intensity a young person may feel about a loss.

The message that caring adults can unconsciously give a young person is that the loss isn't really that important and that if they were more mature (adult), they would handle it better. In this way, many important losses get overlooked. When young people aren't given an opportunity to grieve, they are cheated out of the opportunity to express their feelings and to grow through the loss. The real message is stuff your feelings, take it like an adult, and keep on living.

The Costs of Having a Full Loss Pot

People who experience loss have to sort their way through all of these messages. These messages are a common part of our everyday relationships—common, but not necessarily helpful. They make it very easy to stuff your pain in your loss pot and try to keep on living. However, there are some major costs to pay for dragging a full loss pot through your life.

Remember, like it or not, aware of it or not, people have feelings after a loss. It doesn't matter if they can express them, or even if they are aware of them! Grief is a natural, human response to loss (some people say animals and even plants grieve too). But problems occur when people don't have ways to express their feelings about a loss. Stuffed feelings influence who we are, how we think, and how we see the world. This means there are both short-term and long-term costs to having a full loss pot.

Short-term Costs

In the short run, a full loss pot can mean problems concentrating. As a result, you may not do well in school or at work. You may find that everyone else is harder to get along with, that you have a shorter fuse and are quick to anger. This can lead to problems in your relationships with friends and family. You may be so hard to live with that some people actually go away.

When you stuff your sadness, it creates a general sense of hopelessness. As a result, you may stop caring about your grades, your appearance, your health, or your social life. You may let things slide, not keep up, and gradually drop out.

With enough stuff in your loss pot, you may develop a gloomy world view. You might feel that your family, traffic, teachers, electricity, the earth, and the government are all against you. You

This whole year has been just too crazy for me I guess. If things keep going on the way they are, I am just going to bust out and seriously hurt somebody. I just want everybody to know one thing (that) I am from 62nd St. East Coast Crips and I will always be a Crip no matter how old I get.

—Boy, Sixteen

could feel like there are few if any reasons to be happy, that you have nothing to be thankful for, that no one cares about you, or, worst of all, that you are not lovable.

Anger is a feeling often associated with loss. If you stuff too much anger in a loss pot, you might walk around angry at everybody and everything. This anger under pressure turns you into a bomb looking for a place to explode. Many very angry people commit random acts of violence because somehow they feel justified.

My Loss Pot

*Anger repressed can poison
a relationship as surely as
the cruelest words.*

—Joyce Brothers

People who have all these problems may begin to grow a hard shell over their feelings, a shell so thick that nothing and no one can get to them. They can get lost inside themselves, in their own little world, and use the shell to insulate themselves from the pain and hurt of more losses. They are very hard to get to know and can't really be friends with anyone. People like this, lost inside their full loss pots, will need lots of help and support to break out.

*It's astonishing in this world
how things don't turn out
at all the way you expect
them to!*

—Agatha Christie

Long-term Costs

After years and years of packing losses in the loss pot with no understanding or support, people are changed in deep ways... sometimes forever.

If you have a really full loss pot, a general hopelessness about life in the short run can grow to a long-term "what's the use?" attitude. You may "give up," chronically feel sorry for yourself, and always be angry at the world. This way of looking at things makes it easy to justify totally dropping out. You might become abusive to yourself or others and live in the moment, doing whatever it takes not to feel the huge load of stuffed hurt in your loss pot. You may even stop caring about what happens and do things to hurt yourself.

Sometimes the weight and sadness of a full loss pot is just too much to bear. When that happens, some people will choose one of the thousands of ways to go away, to avoid feeling anything at all. They may use chemicals, or gamble compulsively, or watch TV constantly. To avoid feeling anything at all, they distract themselves from their feelings, no matter what the cost to themselves or others.

People who go through life with full loss pots also tend to be depressed and fearful. Because they have seen so much of the down side of life, they are experts at it. They are fearful because they have had lots of losses, and they expect losses are always going to happen. They keep their guard up constantly. They are not likely to show their real selves out of the fear that someone will disappoint them, let them down, break their heart, or go away. They can become closed up, serious, and mysterious people.

A loss pot can get so full that it will occasionally spill over. This is why some people seem to cry almost instantly and over just about anything. If you find yourself in tears over a Saturday morning cartoon, a flower, a television commercial, even the news, if you are drawn to sad books, sad movies, sad people, or tearful soap operas, it may be a hint that your loss pot is too full.

People can also go the other way and never cry. Someone with a full loss pot may never look under the lid for fear of crying or being overwhelmed by big feelings. For these people, having *any* feelings can be so threatening that they put enormous energy into not having feelings at all. Nothing seems to upset them, no matter how painful it is to

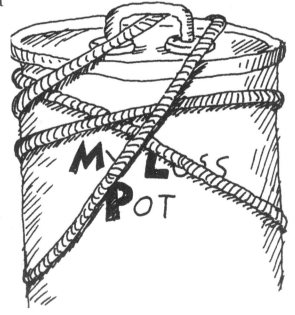

others. These people have shut off their emotions. Unfortunately, this shuts out the good feelings as well as the sad ones.

Keeping the lid on your loss pot means you use your head more because your heart is put away. Because people are cut off from their feelings, they experience the world through their minds. This is why people with full loss pots tend to be more serious and analytical. When they go to a sad movie, they will find it "interesting" and try to figure it out instead of *having* sad feelings. While nothing seems to bother them, they may be putting a lot of effort into looking strong and not showing emotion. Real strength, however, comes from facing your feelings, not holding them back.

All of this means people who have accumulated lots of loss will go through life with a heavy load. They will be less able to be playful, creative, spontaneous, and fun and less open to love. In short, they will be cut off from the part of them they need to be their best and enjoy life to the fullest.

When I was in fourth grade two of my best friends had cystic fibrosis. I grew very close to them over the next few years. When I was in ninth grade, one of my friends died. I personally couldn't cope with it. I missed three days of school. All I could think about is why God would take her and not some maniac. I cried just thinking about it. At her funeral and wake I just bawled my eyes out. Since then, I truly have not been able to think about it and be okay.
—Heidi, Fifteen

A full loss pot can become self-perpetuating. Over time you naturally and unconsciously move toward people who are like you. Just like smokers hang out with smokers, computer people hang with computer people, and people who like the same music hang out together, people with a lot of stuff in their loss pots also have "special interest" groups. Without realizing it, you may have surrounded yourself with others who have full loss pots and who will support you in your downside view of life.

... in order to feel anything you need strength...
—Anna Maria Ortese

Do It Now or Drag It Around

You can choose to deal with your losses as they occur or stuff them for another day. Until you are willing, able, and ready to deal with them, however, they remain in your loss pot, a part of who you are, and they color your view of the world.

Because loss pots fill up so gradually over the years, they can be full of old hurts and sad feelings without your realizing it. That mix of old losses all blended together doesn't go away. It all just sits there in a big sad stew for the rest of your life or until you finally empty it.

Lightening the load in your loss pot means taking on two separate challenges. The first challenge is to get through new losses without stuffing more feelings in your loss pot. Getting through these hard times in the best possible way will require an understanding of the experience of loss so you know what to expect of yourself in each of the different stages of grief. You will also need to know the best ways to take care of yourself on the journey and how to get support for the difficult losses yet to come.

The second challenge is to willingly explore the feelings already in your loss pot. This means talking or writing about the old sadness, sometimes re-experiencing the feelings associated with past losses. It's easier to deal with your old losses now, on your terms, when you are better equipped to handle them. In the section called "Exploring Your Loss Pot" (see page 105), you will learn how to look into your loss pot and begin to undo the old hurts. It is the *only* way to lighten your load.

So let's begin with the first challenge: learning the very important skills for getting through loss and grief.

GETTING THROUGH GRIEF THE BIG PICTURE

So far we have looked at the wide range of experiences that can be considered loss events. We also explored grief, the natural and complicated mix of feelings we experience in response to all losses. We learned that similar feelings occur with all losses, and that the intensity of the feelings and how long it takes to heal changes with the importance of the loss and your skills and resources.

We discovered that because of the emotional intensity losses stir up, some people find ways to avoid experiencing their feelings. When people go away from their feelings, their emotions get stuffed into their loss pot where they cook away forever or until they are taken out and worked through. Finally, we learned that there are some major costs to people who drag full loss pots around all their lives.

In this section, we want to help you understand the big picture of the loss and grief process. As time passes after a loss, people move

43

through many different stages in the process of healing. Each stage is an important, necessary, and natural part of growing through a loss.

In this section, we'll give you a map of the grief process to help guide you through your loss experiences. Maps help you to know where you have been, where you are, and what's ahead. When you're lost in the scary, emotional territory that accompanies a big loss, a map can reduce some of the fear and confusion.

In this section, you will also learn about the basic skills for growing through the hard emotional times. Having skills doesn't mean you avoid the pain and sadness of your losses. It means that you will know how best to take care of yourself as you move through the natural stages of grief and the healing process. Having skills for the hard times means you are more likely to grow, mature, develop strengths, and find the gifts in your loss experience.

The best place to start an exploration of any new territory is to look at the map.

A Map of the Territory

It's possible to map out the different stages of the grieving process, but unlike other maps, the locations on this map tend to move around a bit. Because people are so different when it comes to loss, the stages in the grieving process can vary in intensity, overlap, be revisited, or sometimes not consciously show up at all. Given all those conditions, here is a general map of the territory:

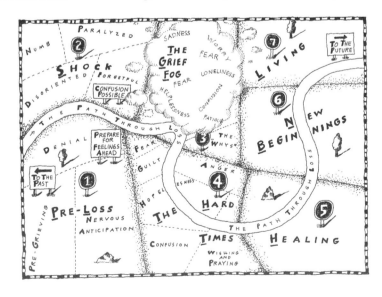

As we explore the places along the way, we'll be adding more details. For now, this is a picture of what lies ahead for a person experiencing an important loss. One example of the uniqueness of a grief map is that it doesn't always start with a loss! Sometimes we can see the loss coming long before it actually happens. That is why the first location on the grief map is called "pre-loss."

Stage 1—Pre-Loss

Many losses don't occur suddenly. Often we can sense or see them approaching. Anticipating a move, watching someone struggle with a long illness, hearing parents talk about separating, or knowing graduation is coming all set us up to expect a change. Like hearing an approaching plane way off in the distance, we get early warnings that something is coming and that our lives are going to be different in some way. Even if it's a positive change, it means that "how it used to be" will end, and that means grieving the loss of the old way.

Because of our many differences, each of us will handle this pre-loss stage very differently. Three general approaches include denial, nervous anticipation, and actual pre-grieving.

Denial

Some people get an early start on ignoring the change, the feelings, and the challenges of facing a future loss. Consciously or unconsciously, they become busy with other parts of life or get overinvolved in activities so they don't have the time or energy to think about or prepare for what's coming. But putting things off merely guarantees more stuff in the loss pot and bigger problems down the road. Sadly, it cheats the person out of the opportunity to get ready for the loss.

The most important thing in dealing with death is admitting to yourself that you might not be okay and then dealing with what you are feeling. Putting it off or trying to distract yourself to forget just doesn't work.

—Mackenzie, Seventeen

Nervous Anticipation

At a slightly more conscious level, some people *kind of* acknowledge that a loss is coming. They experience their feelings for brief moments, get a sample of the strong and complicated emotions waiting for them, and then retreat back into a mild form of denial for protection. Because of the fear and discomfort that gets stirred up, people will flip back and forth between protective denial and nervous anticipation. The coming loss hangs in the background like the soft music that is played continuously in elevators and stores. Sometimes we experience it and sometimes not, it just floats in and out. But if we listen closely, we can sense the feelings of approaching loss and change just below the surface.

Nervously anticipating a loss does give us some chance to prepare. We can talk a little about our feelings when we have the opportunity. We can, in brief moments, consider how our life might be different, test out the feelings of grief, and begin to think about who we'll be able to lean on when we really encounter The Hard Times. Nervous anticipation is how most people cope with a coming loss.

Pre-Grieving

A person who understands the grieving process can actually get ready for loss. This is the most conscious level where a person can prepare for and actually pre-grieve the loss. If you were running a marathon, you wouldn't want to wait until the day before the event to get yourself ready. The same is true for grieving a loss.

Pre-grieving means making time to be with your feelings, starting a journal, or turning up your involvement in your spiritual life. You might consider taking actions that might not be possible after the loss. Things like saying good-byes or "I love you's," taking pictures, and talking about the "old days." You may actually ask your friends to help you through the loss and tell them specifically what type of support you'll be needing.

To prepare for difficult times ahead you might start to take care of yourself by getting plenty of rest, good food, and exercise. These are all things you can do to get ready, *if* you are open to what's coming. Pre-grieving is really first-rate preparation. It reduces the chance of permanent injury and increases the likelihood that you will grow through your losses in the best way possible.

While the best prepared person has real advantages, it is very hard to prepare a heart for the shock and pain of the actual loss. At the end of the pre-loss stage, "it" happens, the loss occurs. This marks the formal beginning of your loss experience.

Stage 2—Shock

Whether you have seen it coming and are prepared or the loss comes on suddenly, the actual event is always disorienting. A small loss can hurt, make you angry, and leave you a little unsure about yourself. A big loss can take your breath away and lay you out flat.

My brother died on New Year's Day. I felt as though I lost a limb. I didn't know how to go on.

—Charles, Seventeen

We tend to assume that the world, the people, and the day-to-day living of our lives will pretty much stay the same. It's always amazing to discover that a big loss really changes things... forever. A death, for example, can be almost impossible to understand intellectually and impossible to cope with emotionally. That is why the moment "it" happens, you and your life are changed, immediately, totally, and deeply. At that moment you will probably be in shock. All you can do is somehow try to take it all in and keep on living.

In the actual moment of the loss, there is no such thing as a normal response. Reactions vary greatly from person to person and with the intensity of the loss. If it's a small loss, you may feel some anger, and maybe some temporary confusion and frustration. If it is a big loss, you will probably be a mess.

Just as the body can be injured in a car accident, for example, a big loss injures your

emotions and your spirit. You can think of it as an injury to your will to live, your hopefulness, and your sense of security. The wound can be so great that your normal ways of thinking and feeling and the usual ways you have handled stress in the past are now suddenly and totally inadequate.

Right after a big loss most people are in a daze. Because they are having so many big feelings at once, they actually don't feel anything. It's like watching a fast spinning merry-go-round. Feelings fly by so fast, changing from moment to moment, that you can't catch any one of them. You'll be laughing one minute and crying the next. This is part of the reason people can feel so crazy after a loss. They really *are* very mixed up inside, and even though it's a *normal* experience of grief, it's not fun.

When you are in shock following a big loss, you don't have feelings, your feelings have you. Because of the intensity of the feelings after a big loss, you are at the mercy of whatever feeling is on top at the moment. A person in this place is emotionally out of control and should feel weird, off the wall, confused, angry, disoriented, moody, silly, strung out, tired, and occasionally ugly.

Right after the loss, people talk about being in shock, numb, not feeling anything, being disoriented, and paralyzed with disbelief. Because the mind is trying hard to comprehend the loss, we sometimes forget the loss has happened for a few minutes and then feel the grief all over again each time we "remember." We may forget we have a body and not remember to eat, drink, or rest. Right after a big loss, it very quickly gets difficult to follow normal routines. Even little decisions can feel completely overwhelming. As time passes, things settle down a bit. That's when the really big feelings begin to show up.

Stage 3—The Grief Fog

As the feelings merry-go-round slows down over time, you begin to have solid feelings for brief periods of time. Instead of the numbness of shock, you now have extended moments of profound sadness, anger, or hopelessness. Reality starts to creep back in and you begin to "have" your feelings one at a time. The full impact of your loss is settling in along with the tremendous

48

emotional confusion that results. This is when you step into the emotional fog of grief.

This stage is like moving slowly in a dense fog. Not sure where you are or what direction you're going, you're feeling lost and just moving. Sadness, confusion, anger, hopelessness, fear, loneliness, embarrassment, fatigue, helplessness, disappointment, resentment, or worry just appear out of nowhere and settle over you.

In this grief fog, with feelings swirling around, you can imagine it would be difficult to keep your life running smoothly. You may have trouble with friends and family members. You lose your sense of what or who is important. You may even find yourself angry at people, traffic, the universe, or the spiritual force in your life for the way things have unfolded.

At about this point, you may find yourself entering "the whys." A person feeling the full sadness/anger/confusion of the loss may begin to ask those difficult and unanswerable ques-

My parents are making me move away from the place I grew up. They did not have to move but my dad wanted to. I was hurt because they didn't care about my feelings. They just wanted more money. I don't know what I'll do. I have not learned how to deal with it yet. For the first five weeks I lost control over myself and didn't care what happened or who I hurt. I was lost. Now I pretend it doesn't hurt, but when I think about it I get angry, scared, and just break down and start crying.

—Michael, Fifteen

I'm still mad at God for taking away my dog, and my parents too for wanting me to get a new one.

—Joel, Twelve

I've lost five or six friends in the last three years because of violence in my community. One of my friends died because of gang violence. The next friend I lost, he was shot by an officer. He was a very close friend and I cared about him. And then there was a girl I have known since fifth grade. She was sitting in a car with a friend over by the grocery store, and while they were sitting there two men approached the car and fired shots in the car injuring him and shot her in the head. They took her to the hospital where she was in a coma, and the doctors said that she was 99.8 percent dead. I mean why does it have to happen to them? They ain't done nothing wrong except try to live in a world that doesn't make any sense.

—Shawnee, Seventeen

tions. Why me? Why now? Why them? Why do I feel so bad? Why didn't I do this or that?... on and on and on. Few satisfactory answers are ever found, but you'll be tempted to wander around in the questions for a time.

It takes a lot of energy to cope with all these feelings and questions floating around. It is easy to feel overwhelmed and exhausted on top of everything else that is going on. When you are worn down physically and emotionally, you're more likely to be sick, have allergies, have difficulty sleeping, not be able to function at school or work, and not even feel like eating.

Because it is so hard to deal with so many different feelings, this is another time where people are tempted to stuff their feelings. The ol' loss pot is off in the distance calling out, "Don't bother with all this emotional mess, just stuff your feelings in me and pretend nothing serious ever happened." You may find yourself wanting to sleep all day (or for the rest of your life) or becoming totally preoccupied with homework, television, music, sports, or food.

Some people even adopt a lighthearted and playful attitude in response to all their pain. It's an example of the many contradictions that occur as a result of all the emotional confusion. Not only do people in the grief fog not quite know who or where they are, they often don't know how to ask for directions.

As time passes, the confusion does begin to lift. Feelings don't fly by so fast, and you can catch your breath. You have time to experience your feelings more individually... more intensely. This is when the full weight of what has happened really comes home. The weight of the painful reality will often drag you to the feelings bottom, and The Hard Times really begin.

Stage 4—The Hard Times

If you're lucky, you will fully experience the painful reality of your loss. You'll be lucky because if you get to this place, it means you're not taking major side trips to avoid your feelings. It also means that you're not busy stuffing feelings into your loss pot to carry around for years. You're also lucky because as you experience The Hard Times, you also experience some major growth. You'll be lucky, but "lucky" is the last thing you will feel... there's a reason it's called The Hard Times.

The Hard Times is the most difficult place to be because it's an emotional bottoming out. The confusion of the grief fog is lifting, all the commotion that immediately followed the loss is quieting down, and now you get to really consider life after your loss. During The Hard Times, your feelings stop coming at you so fast. You now experience each one individually and, as a result, more intensely. A feeling like anger, fear, or self-doubt can become huge, monstrous, and totally overwhelming. It's as though every feeling is being experienced through a giant emotional magnifying glass. Just about any feeling can grab your heart and pull you to the heights, or more often, drag you down into the depths. This is another place where feelings have you, not the other way around.

It doesn't help that by the time you get to The Hard Times you will probably be completely exhausted. Remember, you have been

The day is as dark, as the hollow in my heart
The happiness has been washed away, with nothing left to stay
All I see is an image of a meaningless place
Maybe it's the unspoken sky that tells it all
Or maybe it's the weakness that's been called
The light has been built upon us
And reality is catching up
I must be patient, I must have faith
I must believe in what I have to face
I must survive this endless terror
That awaits for my everyday errors
Whisper of the unknown, echoes through my aching head
Waiting for my unanswered questions to be fed ...
—Shawnee, Seventeen

wounded, were in shock, and then wandered around in an emotional fog for a while. By this time you are extremely tired, emotionally strung out, quite confused, and unsure about how to behave. You are incredibly vulnerable and probably not aware of how emotionally sensitive you've become.

If you are lucky enough to have a map, a few navigational skills, and a safety net of support, you will spend less time in The Hard Times (see "Skills for The Hard Times," page 67). You might be at this emotional bottom for as little as a week or as long as six months. If you find you are in the depths longer than six months, you might need some help to dig out. However long you are there, it will seem like forever.

Having big feelings is difficult and exhausting. When you're really down, it's hard to understand but important to remember that **having powerful feelings is a normal and healthy part of growing through your loss.**

A few of the common, *normal* and large feelings The Hard Times can bring are discussed below.

> **ANGER**—You may have a very short fuse and find yourself angry at life, yourself, those closest to you, the person or object you lost, "the way things are," animals, plants, the earth, air, and "stupid people" everywhere. After a big loss you should be angry—something important has been taken away. While some people express it better than others, anger is normal and a large part of the grief experience.

> **FEAR**—After a big loss, you suddenly realize that nothing is forever and that things can change radically in a blink of an eye. This understanding can make you feel less safe and secure. It is an easy step from here to feeling scared for your own safety or to worrying about the safety of your family, friends, pets, or even strangers. Others may tell you that your fears are a little overdone, but because of the intensity of the feeling, it's hard not to be consumed with fear at times.

> **CONFUSION**—Confusion is also normal after a big loss. Though you wish your world could make sense, during The

Hard Times, everything remains a question mark. Think about it: You have lost something or someone important and experienced the shock of the loss. Then you wandered around in an emotional fog. You kept asking a lot of difficult "why" questions and didn't get any good answers. Given this picture, it's easy to see that a person could be confused and uncertain about things.

At the bottom, you live with a confused sense of who you are and what's important. This confusion is frustrating and uncomfortable. Yet it's the *natural* result of the mind, body, emotions, and spirit taking a time-out to reorganize.

While it may be a normal and healthy part of healing, confusion is not a condition most people tolerate very well. In comparison to The Hard Times, our daily life is very orderly and predictable. But after a big loss, confusion is a normal response.

GUILT—Another common and haunting feeling during The Hard Times is that somehow we should have done things differently. We start "if-only"-ing ourselves big time. "If only I'd have done this" or "If only I'd have been there... said something." "If only, if only, if only"... until, in our self-imposed guilt, we actually begin to feel responsible.

It is very unlikely, given all the things that contribute to a loss, that you are so powerful as to be *the* cause of the loss. But lots of people say that after a big loss they felt responsible in some way. While the people that care about you will tell you it just isn't so, you may continue to feel responsible because you can't find any other explanation. The feeling is so strong that other people's opinions just don't carry much weight.

My first big loss was when my Situ (Grandmother in Lebanese) died. I was eleven and it was the first funeral I attended. I was sad to lose her, but her death was a blessing. She had suffered for a year in the hospital. It was especially hard on me since one of the reasons she got worse was because I got sick. I was diagnosed with leukemia when I was ten. She took it very hard and gave up the fight. I miss my Situ but I know she is at peace and that she is watching over me and my family. It took a few years to really stop missing Situ all the time. Now I know she is living in my heart and that she is watching over me.

—Jessica, Seventeen

53

My first big loss occurred a little less than a year ago. I was fourteen years old when my dog was hit and killed by a car. To some this incident might be minor, but so far in my life I've been fortunate enough for this to be my first big loss. When I found out what had happened, I immediately blamed myself ... "I shouldn't have let her out," "I should have been kinder to her."

—Omeed, Fifteen

You can wish you'd have expressed more love or been more careful. We all will have regrets and we always could have done more. But when you feel guilty and think you are actually responsible for a loss, you are going too far. You are deepening your own wound. It may be irrational but guilt is a common response to a big loss.

WISHING AND PRAYING—In the moments when we are really in The Hard Times, it is natural to wish life was different... like it used to be. We may create an idealized view of the past and try to live in our fantasy, pretending things never changed, that the loss never happened. You may wish it's all a bad dream and that you are going to wake up and find yourself back to normal. If you didn't have a faith life, you may develop one and pray for things to be different. Wishing and praying things were different are normal and natural responses to your loss.

HEAVY GRAVITY—If you're not taking care of yourself physically and emotionally, The Hard Times will be totally exhausting. After running an emotional marathon, your body and spirit will be wrung out. Sick, tired, sick and tired, it can feel like the gravity on the planet has doubled. Just getting up and moving around can take enormous effort. Your desire to do things, go out, or even change channels can drop to zero. You may actually find yourself staring at a terrible station on TV because it is too much work to change it and anyway, "It just doesn't matter."

HOPELESSNESS—When it doesn't get better, and you don't wake up from the bad dream, and it feels like you've been on the bottom forever, and you're exhausted, and your prayers aren't answered, and you're confused, tired, and angry, and people just don't understand, and you're feeling alone with it all... hopelessness is a normal response.

You have to be careful here though. *Too much* hopelessness and despair is *not* normal. Unfortunately you will be the last person who's a good judge of how much is too much. If you **even have a hint that you have gone over the edge with hopelessness, get help immediately.** Thoughts of ending it all, feeling out of control, feeling a lot of fear, feeling totally isolated, or using drugs to mask your pain are all signals you desperately need help and support. None of these feelings or behaviors move you in the direction of healing.

Trying to be "strong" as you spiral down the drain is ridiculous and self-destructive. **The "strong" people are those who know when they are up against more than they can cope with and reach out for help.** Don't wait, ask for help.

After you have struggled through the difficult experiences in The Hard Times, your wound will eventually begin to heal. One day, after being on the bottom for what seems like forever, an absolutely amazing thing happens. Suddenly you realize you have just had a couple of hours of feeling pretty good. Or you find yourself laughing a real laugh or being excited about something new and you realize that for brief moments in time you *are* feeling better. You are not out of the woods yet, still much more down than not, but you have started to heal. After the bottom, believe it or not, it gets continually better.

Stage 5—Healing

From those first few moments when you sense relief, things get gradually better. The healing stage can take anywhere from three to eighteen months. As your healing process unfolds, the wound of your loss is gradually beginning to close. The periods when you feel like a normal human, with some optimism and energy, gradually lengthen. You and the people around you will sense the difference, that you are changing in important ways.

However, healing means "getting better," not fixed. The struggle in you is still being waged. This is a time when you *gradually* begin to let go of the past and begin to accept the new reality. You are moving from resisting your difficult grief feelings to accepting them as a natural consequence of your loss. As your acceptance grows, the possibility of your survival and life beyond your loss begins to appear.

In the healing stage there will still be dark times, sometimes even long excursions back to The Hard Times. These retreats are *not* failures or signs that you will never get better. They are simply evidence that your healing process needs more time. Grief and healing will not be rushed. The body, mind, emotions, and spirit all have their own special needs for recovering from a loss, and they recover in their own time.

I always entertain great hopes.

—Robert Frost

The moments of sunshine should give you hope. You should consider them evidence that you have rounded a corner and are headed in a new direction. The healing stage marks a turning point when you have begun to let go of the past, have survived the dark present, and are beginning to look forward to a brighter future.

Stage 6—New Beginnings

Eventually, the tide turns. At some point, you'll realize you are having more up days than down. You will actually feel like a normal human most of the time. Like a butterfly that has spent months in a dark cocoon, you are emerging from your grief and opening up to the light. Changed by your experience and feeling new strength, you are getting ready to come back into the life you once called normal.

Your understanding and emotional acceptance of your loss, yourself, other people, and your life all continue to improve. Life begins
to make sense again. Your physical energy and health are improving.
You are sleeping better, eating more normally again, and getting
used to both new and familiar routines. You and your life are getting
put back together.

> *Chaos demands to be recog-
> nized and experienced
> before letting itself be con-
> verted into a new order.*
>
> —Hermann Hesse

With your renewed energy and optimism, you may even consider
new activities, think about new friendships, and begin to have new
dreams for yourself. You may even feel occasional excitement as a
result. This is all a natural part of coming back and opening up to
the world that has been waiting for you all along.

There will still be moments of deep sadness, but they and the
other feelings associated with your loss just won't be as intense and
all consuming. Some people even cherish these moments as opportunities to honor the importance of the loss in their life. Occasional
feelings of anger, fear or confusion or the "whys" will still float by,
but they won't demand as much of your energy or attention.

> *Although the world is full of
> suffering, it is full also of the
> overcoming of it.*
>
> —Helen Keller

At this point you are reaching, stretching, and rapidly becoming
the new you. The person who has been changed, sometimes deeply,

58

sometimes in small ways, is getting ready to step forward, to take flight.

Stage 7—Living

One day you realize it has been a long time since you last thought about your loss. This can happen as much as a year to three years after a big loss, but the time does arrive.

The new you is launched. You are back in the rush of daily life, your old life, and some new people, projects, goals, and challenges. With more energy and a positive attitude, you've re-entered normal living. That means normal problems, struggles, joys, and sadness, but nothing that compares to the emotional intensity of your big loss experience.

For a while, when I was getting better, I got mad at myself because I thought it meant I didn't care anymore that my brother had died. Then I realized I was just getting better.
—Becky, Fifteen

In the depth of winter, I finally learned that within me there lay an invincible summer.

—Albert Camus

But you have been changed. Now a movie, a song, or someone else's loss experience can quickly take you back to the memory of what you've been through. In the place in you that knows about loss, you will feel a stirring of familiar feelings. Your experience with loss has made you a deeper person, more sensitive to loss and grief in your own life as well as in others. Like the tree that adds a ring of growth every year, you've added another dimension. You have grown and matured.

During the churning in the depths of your grief, over and over again you asked the hard questions about yourself and your life. As a result, you may find you are operating with a new sense of who you are, what you are capable of, and what is really important in your life. A new "you" almost always results if you can successfully get through The Hard Times.

59

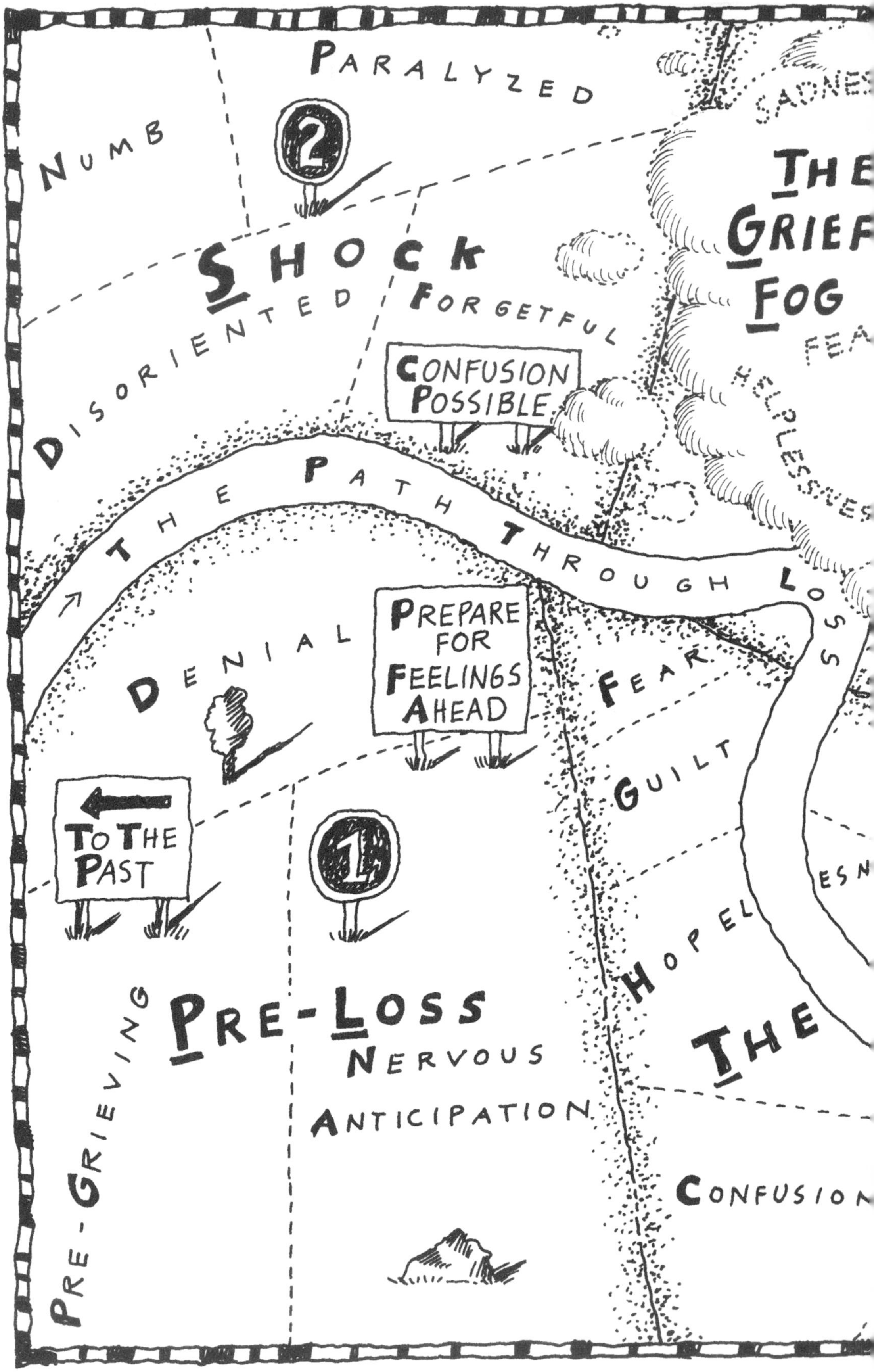

PARALYZED

NUMB

②

SHOCK

DISORIENTED   FORGETFUL

SADNES

THE
GRIEF
FOG

FEA

CONFUSION
POSSIBLE

HELPLESSNES

→ THE PATH THROUGH LOS

DENIAL

PREPARE
FOR
FEELINGS
AHEAD

FEAR

GUILT

←
TO THE
PAST

①

HOPEL   ESN

PRE-LOSS
NERVOUS

ANTICIPATION

PRE-GRIEVING

THE

CONFUSION

WORRY

FEAR

LONELINESS

CONFUSION

FATIGUE

THE "WHYS"

ANGER

LIVING

⑦

TO THE FUTURE

⑥

NEW BEGINNINGS

④

HARD

⑤

THE PATH THROUGH LOSS

TIMES

HEALING

WISHING AND PRAYING

GROWING THROUGH THE HARD TIMES

Now that you have an understanding of the "normal" stages in the grief process and some idea of what to expect along the way, the next step is to learn how to take care of yourself at each stage. This means learning about the special skills and resources for each part of the journey. Getting through The Hard Times is all about understanding the territory and then developing and using special skills.

If you are experiencing a big loss or even a not-so-big one right now, you may not be in a mood to read a lot. Here is a quick list of

some of the really important things to know or remember as you go through your grief process. It's like first aid, how to take care of yourself in an emergency until you can get to more help.

> *Sadness is related to the opening of your heart. If you allow yourself to feel sad, especially if you can cry, you will find that your heart opens more and you can feel more love.*
>
> —*Shakti Gawain*

Seven Things a Grieving Person Needs to Know

1. YOU ARE LOVABLE EVEN WHEN YOU ARE A CONFUSED MESS— Feeling down, alone, sad all the time, cranky, moody, tired, hopeless, angry, confused, and worse doesn't mean you are a failure as a human being. In fact it means quite the opposite: You are a normal and healthy young person. You are feeling what you *should be* feeling after a big loss. Your unhappiness is an expression of your humanness. You may be down but you are still a competent, lovable person deserving of others' care and respect, not to mention being nice to yourself.

2. CRYING IS A GIFT—It's the people who can't cry who lose out. They are cheated out of this way of expressing a basic human emotion. Your tears honor your loss and your humanness. It is how you

know your Loss was important. Tears also help you relieve pent-up emotional pressure in a healthy way. Crying is a gift and tears help us to know we are alive. **It's okay to cry until the need to cry goes away by itself.**

3. *ALMOST* EVERY THOUGHT, FEELING, AND BEHAVIOR IS NORMAL—With big and not-so-big losses, people's lives can get pretty scrambled up. That is why it is common for people to be, think, or feel weird at times. Being depressed, quick to anger, weird in your humor, or wildly happy at odd times are all fairly common for grieving people. As long as your behavior is not illegal or self-destructive and doesn't go on for too long, you are probably pretty normal in spite of how you feel or appear.

4. YOU ARE NOT ALONE—For whatever comfort it may provide, people have been grieving their hearts out since the beginning of time, and surviving. At any given moment somewhere on the planet, hundreds of thousands of young people are going through the same kinds of pain you are experiencing. You are not alone; people understand; you will get through it.

5. PEOPLE ARE UNCOMFORTABLE WITH GRIEVING

PEOPLE—Other people's loss pots get stirred up by just being around a grieving person. This can cause some people to be sympathetic and supportive and cause others to be very uncomfortable and simply go away. People may not even realize they are avoiding you, but by doing so they are avoiding their own uncomfortable feelings.

Because most people don't know much about the grief process, it's hard for them to know how to be helpful. When your co-worker, friend, or family member has just had a big loss and is moody, it can be difficult to know what to say or how to offer support. It's easier to just ignore the whole thing.

It is not helpful to blame someone who won't, can't, or doesn't know how to be there for you. It's better to find other people who can support you and to be as clear as you can about what you need from them. **It's important to remember that if people are uncomfortable with your grief, it's their problem.** You need to be true to yourself. Don't try to ignore your feelings in order to make others comfortable. Find the people who can understand and will accept you and your grief.

6. NO MATTER HOW BAD YOU FEEL

YOU WILL SURVIVE—No matter what your loss, millions of people have had losses just like yours and survived. While you and your experience of a loss are unique, all those people have suffered pretty much like you, and they got through it. Your grief makes you human. You can get through it. Basically, your only options are to run from the complicated feelings or to face your loss and get through it. You can carry your wound through your life or you can help it to heal cleanly. But you will survive and grow from this experience no matter how you feel right now.

7. IT TAKES AS LONG AS IT TAKES—As you slowly move through the predictable stages of healing from a big loss, there will come a time when you are tired of feeling down. There will be a day when you say, "I'm tired of this grief stuff and I want it to be over." You will feel like you can't take another day of being sad, serious, tired, teary, confused, and on your own with it all. You'll wonder if you have been changed permanently in some way and begin to fear that the grief will never lift. These are all normal feelings.

Unfortunately, **healing takes as long as it takes** and having a tantrum will not hurry it along. Remember that you are healing from a major physical, mental, emotional, and spiritual wound. Just like that little cut on your finger, the wound from your loss *will* heal naturally and in its own time. Your job is to take great care of yourself in the meantime.

Skills for The Hard Times

Knowing how to take care of yourself in the meantime is the art of growing through loss. Big losses demand more of us than the not-so-big and small losses, but all losses take us on a similar journey. When you are experiencing the shock of a big loss and are temporarily lost in an emotional fog, you are usually not able to think about how to take care of yourself. At those times, your feelings are in control, and thinking about self-care is pretty hard. When you come out of the grief fog to face the reality of your loss, The Hard Times begin. It's at that point when self-care skills become really important. Self-care skills can make the difference between a grief wound that refuses to heal and one that heals cleanly.

Every culture, ethnic tradition, and spiritual orientation approaches loss differently and has special resources to offer the grieving person. But there are also some things that apply to grieving people everywhere. From the following list of suggestions for negotiating The Hard Times, pick the actions that feel right for you.

Don't compromise yourself.
You are all you've got.

—Janis Joplin

• **DON'T "DO" ANYTHING**—The most important self-care ability for this stage is actually a "nonaction." To grow through these hard times, to have your hurts heal cleanly, and to not create new problems, don't do anything to feel better. Another way to say that is "don't run from the hurt." As unpleasant as it feels, the discomfort is a normal, natural, and necessary part of your healing process.

Sometimes, as a way to get relief from our discomfort, we are tempted to want to "get away from it all," to "do something" about feeling so bad. If you act on these understandable impulses you may regret your decisions later. While actions like moving, changing jobs, giving your stuff to others, running away, changing relationships, buying things, taking drugs, or quitting school might seem like they would lead to some relief, all they really do is temporarily create a distraction. They also create more change in the present and can result in bigger problems down the road.

Change is why you are emotionally confused in the first place. Don't add to the burden by creating more. Try not to make any big decisions within the first six months to a year following a major loss. As uncomfortable as you are, the best way to cope with The Hard Times is by going through, not around, your feelings of grief.

• **REMEMBER, GRIEF IS NORMAL AND HEALTHY—** Millions of other people have had similar losses and survived. Grieving, even feeling miserable, is normal, necessary, and a natural part of the healing process. Just as nature provides for seasons of the year, there is a natural order to the "seasons" in the grief process. Your springtime will come.

• **DON'T TRY TO KEEP IT ALL TOGETHER—**To a degree, it is necessary to "come apart" when you've had a big loss. Your life is being rearranged as a result of your loss, and you are also being reorganized. Although it may not be comfortable, it's normal to have big feelings, be absent-minded, act strange, and feel uncertain and unsure about how your life will unfold. The skill is not so much to fix this condition but to accept it as a natural response to a big loss. The challenge is to be patient with yourself while the natural healing process runs its course.

• **IF YOU NEED HELP, GET IT—** With a big loss, something important has been taken away and deep sadness is natural. At times you might even feel like it's too much effort to go on. If you are drowning in your feelings of grief, ask for a life preserver. Only in the movies can heroes and heroines handle their problems alone. That's because it's the movies and not real life. Psychologically healthy people, even those who are up to their ears in loss and grief, are able to say, "I can't..." or "I don't want to handle this alone." And then they will reach out for help.

• **BE YOURSELF NO MATTER WHAT—**Because everyone is different, there is no "normal" way to grieve. Whatever you feel or think is okay, acceptable, forgivable. You don't have to explain yourself. Your feelings and thoughts don't

have to be logical; in fact, they can even be downright irrational. For example, lots of people find humor and laughter
at the bottom of the bottom where you'd least expect it.
Happiness in the middle of heavy grieving doesn't mean
the loss wasn't important. It is a reminder that grief is not
one emotion but many different feelings going on in you in
the same moment. At times, your mind and heart need a
rest from the heaviness and a little laughter pops up. When
you're in The Hard Times though, it just doesn't last long.

Whatever happens, just be you. Don't feel guilty or self-
conscious about any feelings. Whatever you feel after a big
loss is just you being you and trying to cope. Self-love and
self-acceptance are gifts you can give yourself when you
are experiencing an enormous emotional injury.

• **CRY IF YOU CAN**—If you can cry you are really lucky.
Some people think that crying is a sign of weakness, but
actually the opposite is true. Stuffing your feelings into
your loss pot is what makes you a depressed and serious
person. That is when you really become weak and vulnerable.

One of the best things to do when you experience even
a little sense of loss or grief is to give yourself permission
to cry. Crying releases pent-up emotional pressure. It's a
very healthy way to express your feelings. Crying
often helps when you can't find the words
you need, or words can't fully convey
what you're feeling.

Crying doesn't have to make sense
or be good timing. You can cry alone
or with a good friend, a parent, or even
a counselor who will be understanding. If others have a problem with tears, let *them* be
uncomfortable. Cry when it comes and cry
until you're done crying. It is the self-respecting thing to do, and it honors your loss. Crying
is a gift.

Tears are like rain. They loosen up our soil so we can grow in different directions.

—*Virginia Casey*

• **TAKE CARE OF YOUR BODY**—The bigger the loss, the bigger the physical and emotional drain. You can be so busy coping, so preoccupied with your grieving, that you don't realize you are running out of energy. It's very much like running a marathon. If you don't take care of yourself along the way, taking water at the aid stations, you can suddenly run out of fuel. It's called hitting the wall. The same thing is true on a long and demanding grief journey. If you don't care for yourself, you will gradually wear down and become exhausted.

Take naps, and go to bed early instead of spending long hours staring at the TV. Take long walks or work out regularly, eat healthy food, go easy on caffeine, and drink lots of water. These simple actions are all ways to help you make it through The Hard Times.

• **KEEP IT SIMPLE**—With all the confusion inside, you'll want to keep a simple and restful schedule for dealing with your outside life. Try not to take on any new responsibilities or activities or complicate your life unnecessarily. A regular and easy schedule of activities means you won't have to make a lot of decisions. If your life is relatively calm and orderly, you'll have more energy for coping with your grief and the confusion inside.

• **LET TIME PASS**—After a big loss it can take months or longer for things to settle down. The time you spend in The Hard Times depends on the importance of your loss. You feel worse if your pet dies than if you lose your English

notebook. After some losses your life is changed forever and will never get completely back to "how it used to be."

Often people will be tired of feeling so bad and be ready for the grief to end long before it does. Grieving people often ask, "When is it going to be over?" or "Will this ever end?" The answer is *yes*, your grieving *will* ease up and your ability to function will improve. But for now you should simply remember grief is not something we "do" or have control over. It just happens, and **grief gets better in its own time.**

Skills for growing through the hard times are mostly about how to take good care of yourself while you *naturally* go through the process of healing. Taking care of yourself, being very patient, and letting time pass are all that is required. When you are patient, when you let time pass, you are "doing something" important.

Who Was There for You in Your Grief?

My friends were there. They sat and listened to me. Told me to blow it off.

—Angela, Eighteen

No one was there. I was alone.

—Eric, Fifteen

My best friends, Jack Daniels and Jim Beam.

—Nick, Sixteen

My parents were really great. Totally patient with me when I was really moody.

—Sean, Sixteen

My brother helped me because we both experienced the same tragedy.

—Reace, Fifteen

I learned the street way, that you have to look out for yourself and no one else, because no one's looking out for you.

—Shawnee, Seventeen

I lost my grandpa Erve when I was eight. I felt really bad because when he called a few days before he died I didn't talk to him. When it happened it made me hug my other grandpa even tighter. My family and I comforted each other and it helped that my friends were so caring. I knew I would make it and I did.

—Lindsey, Ten

• **BE WITH CARING PEOPLE**—What would you think if you saw someone who had just had an accident, who was having difficulty walking, had torn clothing, had black-and-blue eyes, was bleeding like mad, and refused help or medical attention? Nuts, right? When you are in The Hard Times you're like that person. You are nursing deep emotional wounds. After a big loss you may be handling daily life, even looking okay on the outside, but inside you're hurt pretty bad. Allowing others to support you can ease the pain and help you to get through it all. It is why we have friends. Friendships actually get stronger when you give people an opportunity to be there for you in difficult moments.

Caring family, friends, and other people can be there for you through the big waves of feeling angry, fearful, confused, and guilty. They will let you know when they think you've gone too far in your feelings, thinking, or behavior. They can help you see the upside of yourself and your life. Most important, they will let you know they care about you, even when you are moody, grouchy, or off the wall.

• **TALK, TALK, TALK—** During The Hard Times there is a lot going on inside you. After a big loss, your whole world has been rearranged. You will have feelings about it, big questions, troublesome thoughts and memories to process. You *need* to talk and talk and talk. You need to let the pressure out.

You will be considering and reconsidering questions about your loss. You will need a very special group of listeners, people who will put up with your repetition, who can hear about your pain and not go away. These aren't always easy people to find. Not everyone is wired for patience and emotional intensity. This doesn't mean people don't care; it's just that everyone has limits around what they can tolerate. For example, your friends or family members who've experienced the same loss may not be your best listeners. They will have their own grief issues to work through and may not be able to be there for you.

A good strategy for taking care of your need to keep talking about your loss is to rely on a lot of different people. Spend a little time talking with each of your friends. The important thing to remember is to share your story. You *need* to talk and you *are* worth listening to.

• **GET A GUIDE**—In any confusing territory it's important to find people who are familiar with the terrain. As you will learn, you can get a special kind of support from people who have had a similar loss. Seek these people out; get them to share their experiences; ask them for regular contact. They know a lot about what you are going through. They will make excellent guides through the dark times and difficult places.

A great place to find guides is in a loss support group. In these caring circles, people build trust in each other and come together to help each other get through The Hard Times. In this kind of group we find out that even at our worst, we are more like everyone else than we ever imagined. If you can find a caring and trusting group of listeners, take advantage of it—it's a real gift.

• **ASK FOR SUPPORT**—If you have found a few people who you trust will be there for you, use them. Ask them for their patience and understanding, for regular affirmations, for an occasional hug or to take you out for dinner. You can ask them to put up with your talking and talking and talking about your losses, or for help with especially difficult times like

anniversaries, holidays, or events that you know will stir up your grief.

Being there for each other is what friends are for. Helping a hurting friend is an opportunity for your relationship to grow (see "How to Support a Grieving Person," page 101). You may not always get the response you'd like, but by asking, you create the opportunity for people to be there for you.

• **TAKE SOME TIME ALONE**—Solitude means taking time away for rest and peace of mind. Time to think, cry, do nothing, be quiet, pray, meditate, draw, stare at the TV, or write in your journal. Time alone can help you cope with and heal from your loss. But there is an important difference between solitude and isolation.

Solitude is taking time out; isolation is going away. When we isolate ourselves, we cut ourselves off from others. In doing so we lose the caring and objectivity that being connected to others provides. In isolation, our worst fears and craziest thinking about ourselves and life spools up without the perspective of others for balance. In isolation, no one is around to say, "I know you feel hopeless now, but I love you and will stick with you as long as you need me."

Taking time for ourselves helps, but cutting ourselves off from others is how we can deepen our wounds and prolong our healing. *Getting away* from it all is how we rest and can be alone with our thoughts and memories. *Going away* from it all is how we injure ourselves.

• **LEAN ON YOUR SPIRITUALITY**—The planets orbit, the earth turns, seasons change, lives change, beings come into the world and they go. Change and endings are the natural order of things. We just forget all that because loss hurts.

Your understanding of how the universe works may be helpful in times of major losses. Any faith in a spiritual force like God, the Tao, the Universal Consciousness, Nature, the Great Spirit, the Natural Order of Things, or whatever you experience as a power greater than yourself operating in the universe can be a nurturing and supportive resource when you are grieving.

As a Christian I know that there is no loss too great to handle. God will never give you anything you can't cope with. That isn't to say that all losses should be dealt with alone—there is help when you need it. But, I've learned through experience that the best way to sort through the damage (emotional and physical) done by loss is with prayer.
—Summer, Seventeen

> **Sometimes I go about pitying myself, and all the time I am being carried on great winds across the sky.**
>
> *—Ojibway saying*

In moments of great pain we often feel overwhelmed by the power of big changes. Sometimes it is very hard to comprehend why things happen the way they do. With big changes we always ask the enormous question of "why?" Why me, why now, why them... and more unanswerable questions. In those moments we can lean on our spirituality to help us believe there is an answer to the "why" that is too big for our understanding, and then to yield to the pain of it all. Your faith can help you to let go of the details, release your confused and tired mind, and relax into knowing that somehow things are as they should be.

At fifteen life had taught me undeniably that surrender, in its place, was as honorable as resistance, especially if one had no choice.

—Maya Angelou

Because of the power and drama of big losses, many people discover that they want to acquire, reconsider, or deepen a faith life. It can be a powerful and positive resource for growing through the hardest times.

HEALING

If The Hard Times is a dark and overcast day, the healing stage is when the sun occasionally shines through. You are beginning to have moments when you feel like your old self and are looking forward to the future. The healing stage is a middle ground, you're not as down as you were and not yet back to "normal." That means you'll still want to be taking good care of yourself. The following are some special ways to care for yourself in the healing stage.

Skills for Healing

• **LET MORE TIME PASS**—As you begin to heal and feel better, your impatience with being down will also grow. But being impatient with yourself will not help. The length of the healing process depends on many factors, none of which are controlled by you. Usually it varies with the importance and intensity of the loss. A loss is like a physical wound, and it simply takes the time it needs to get better. After a big loss, like it or not, you'll be healing for a long time.

> *Patience is the key to paradise.*
>
> —*Turkish proverb*

• **STAY CALM AND REST**—You can't (and shouldn't try to) prematurely end your grief experience by getting on with your life. You are moving through the *necessary* stages of a healing process. When you get a taste of feeling better you'll naturally want more. You may be inclined to hurry out and get into projects, new relationships, or a flurry of activities before you are really ready. Anything you do to rush the process will only prolong your recovery. Healing is really just being patient and resting while your body, mind, and spirit gradually recover from the shock of your loss.

• **FOCUS ON THE UPSIDE**—By the time you are beginning to heal, you'll have been down a long time. You'll be ready to feel better. The times when you feel "normal," with energy and a good attitude, will come more often and be wonderful. It can also be disappointing when they fade and you move back into your grief. The healing pattern is erratic and different for each person. In down moments it is important to remember that these retreats do not mean your grief will never end. Try to focus on the up times; they signal that your grief is lifting and that the natural healing process is working.

• **BE OPTIMISTIC**—As you heal, your optimism will also grow. You'll be better able to think about living again. Ask someone you like and trust to help you make a list of what is wonderful about you and your life. In The Hard Times it can be difficult or impossible to see the positive aspects of your life and even yourself. As you are healing, you'll have more willingness and ability to see the good things, to see that life isn't so bad after all. Having that list can shorten your retreats to The Hard Times.

---

*I thank you God for this most
amazing day; for the leaping
greenly spirits of trees
and a blue true dream of sky;
and for everything
which is natural which is infinite
which is yes.*

—E. E. Cummings

• **BE NICE TO YOURSELF**—Remember, you're still quite vulnerable. Think about how you would treat a friend just back from the hospital after major surgery. That pretty much describes your condition, just getting over a major trauma and recovering your health. You're better but not "fixed." What do you need as a recovering person?

Continue to get plenty of rest, good food, and exercise. In addition to rebuilding your health, you'll be establishing healthy living patterns. But you should also pamper yourself. Eat some ice cream, take naps and hot baths, whatever makes you feel good. The world will be there when you are ready to be a full player. For now, be nice to yourself.

• **TAKE TIME FOR YOUR MEMORIES—You'll heal sooner and better by working through your grief rather than running from it.** This approach takes courage and good support because it means consciously moving toward uncomfortable feelings. You can do this in many ways: write about your loss in a journal, keep important pictures or favorite objects around, go to familiar places, eat special foods, and even linger in those happy/sad memories of how it used to be. It's okay to hold on to memories as long as you want to... until you are ready to let go. There is no "normal," and almost anything you do is okay.

I kept my dad's cologne in my drawer for two years after he died before I tossed it out. The smell of it kept him in my heart. It made me feel like he was still in the room. I wish I still had it.

—Kelly, Eighteen

• **HONOR THE ENDINGS**—Rituals that help bring closure, that mark our transitions, can be very helpful in our healing. A funeral is the first thing that comes to mind in the case of a death loss. It is a ritual that gets people together, encourages them to share their grief, and marks the transition. They are often complicated and involve a lot of planning.

But you can also create your own activities that will help with closure. You can do them on your own or with others; they can be simple or elaborate. What all closure activities should have in common is that they should be comfortable for those involved, honor losses, mark the passing of the old way, and help your healing process.

Closure Activities

Write letters to people who have gone out of your life.

At a holiday gathering, set a place at the table,
have a picture in a visible place, or name a loved one
who has died in a prayer.

Have a ceremony to talk, laugh, and cry about a pet
that has left your life. Show pictures, tell stories, name
what you will miss, and say good-bye.

Take an hour each month, on the anniversary day
of a loss, to handle objects, look at photos, or to write
about your loss experience.

Visit a grave or the scene of an accident
to leave flowers.

In a journal, write about memories
that have been stirred up as a result
of your loss experience.

Make an anonymous donation
in honor of your loss to an organization
you feel is important.

Plant a tree or flowers to honor
the occasion of a loss.

Yes, closure activities will stir up your loss feelings again. But in doing so intentionally, you are cleaning your emotional house. You will make sure that you're not putting anything in the loss pot. It's like taking an old bandage off of a cut, washing the wound, and then putting on a fresh bandage. It hurts a little when you do, but that's how you ensure the wound heals cleanly. Getting through loss is about experiencing your feelings, not avoiding or running from them. **Actively honoring the endings can help.**

• **THINK ABOUT WHAT IS REALLY IMPORTANT**—When people have a big loss, their lives are often thrown into chaos. What was really important the minute before the loss is suddenly not important at all. Often our day-to-day worries and concerns become unimportant and our connections to other people become very important.

Out of the confusion of a major loss may come big questions about your life and what is really important. How you relate to friends and family may change because you feel that closeness to others has become a higher priority. You may decide to be healthier, quit smoking, or take up a new hobby or interest. You might get another pet or decide never to have a pet again.

The healing stage is a good time to ask yourself, Who am I now? How do I want to put myself and my life back together? If you listen to yourself during your quiet times, as you talk with others, or in looking back on the writings in your journal, you may see a new self emerging.

The opportunity to redesign our lives as a result of a big loss is one of the gifts that can come out of this difficult experience. The increasing optimism of the healing stage makes it a good time to think about who you are going to be and how you're going to live.

• **CREATE SOME STRUCTURE**—In The Hard Times we were challenged with getting through the big feelings. It was important to keep things simple so we could focus inward. In the healing stage we have a little more energy and a better attitude. This can be a good time to begin to give your life a little more structure, to consciously build in time for the important things, and to purposely put things back together.

Create a routine that allows time for important people, a chance to nap, time to write, a little exercise, meditation, and time to be alone. It doesn't have to be elaborate, just enough structure to bring a sense of balance to your life. If you are recovering from a big loss, you will have been through some pretty scattered and disorienting times. The stability and predictability of a little structure can increase your sense of moving toward a "normal" life.

• **CONTINUE TO EXPRESS YOUR GRIEF**—It is amazing how quickly after a major loss everyone else in the world goes back to living a normal life. You, however, are left with your grief. Because everyone else is getting on with it,

the temptation is to pretend you are too. Initially you may try to be like everyone else and fit in. **But pretending you're okay is a lot of work when you are still grieving.** If you are still healing, you *need* to continue to have and express feelings. You'll need to continue to talk about your

experience long after most of your friends have gone on with their lives and forgotten about your loss.

In the healing stage, it's still very important to be with people who have huge ears, skilled listeners who will let you continue to talk, talk, talk. Support groups can be a positive way to indulge this necessary healing process. **Remember, you need to keep talking until the need to talk goes away by itself.**

• **KEEP A JOURNAL**—Often we don't really know what we're feeling till we try to express ourselves to someone else. In a journal you can "catch" and linger with important but fleeting memories, release powerful feelings, and express your deepest and most private thoughts. You can write beautiful poetry out of your pain or write ugly, angry things you really wouldn't want to say to anyone. All of this will contribute to your healing.

. . . and as the sun set on that terrible day, I heard it. The deep low wailing. The cry of all men who had lost fathers that day or ever. And I added mine to the song.

—Anonymous

A journal will become a historical record of your journey out of The Hard Times and your movement back to a normal life. When you look back in your journal, you will be able to see the changes and the progress you have made.

A journal is also a great place to put special memories that you want to come back to later. It's a holding place that you can return to any time you feel the need. Even if your journal sits on the shelf for years, whenever you open it you'll be taken right back to the important memories you never want to forget.

During the healing stage, you are putting yourself and your life back together. Your journal can be like a builder's notebook. It can be where you try out ideas, plans, dreams—where you write about possibilities for the life you are creating.

• **DON'T OVERDO GRIEF**—Sometimes people actually feel guilty about healing. As they feel the energy returning, they worry that it means they don't care about the loss anymore. You will always remember a big loss. You will always be able to go immediately back to the place in your heart where you can feel some of the pain the big loss created. Big losses change us forever. Healing only means that the intensity of what you feel decreases, the confusion clears, your energy returns, and a new you heads back into your life. But you will always care and, at some level, never forget.

If you feel your grief is too deep or has been going on too long, you might want to seek out help. Remember that reaching out for help is a psychologically healthy act. While some things about the grief process are predictable, there is no "normal." If you are uncomfortable with your process, go talk to someone you trust.

• **SAVOR THE BEAUTY IN GRIEVING**—It may sound strange, but people will talk about a beauty or comfort in sorrow. Lingering in sweet memories of "how it used to be," writing passionate poetry out of your grief, taking time out of your normally busy life just to be and feel and think about what was and will be important are all very special opportunities that can come with a loss experience. Being open to these special moments is another way to honor our loss and to linger in the humanness of the experience.

87

• **CONTINUE TO BE PATIENT**—Being patient is not just a state of mind, it is something you can actually do. In those moments when you feel your anger, when you are so tired of not feeling better, or when you're tempted to put yourself down for not getting better faster, you can choose a more positive action: *being* patient.

There are a number of actions you can take when you're feeling restless and impatient: You can call a friend and talk about it, get some exercise, write about impatience in your journal, sit down and meditate, make a list of the things in your life you are grateful for, or simply take a nap. After a big loss, it's normal to be impatient with grief. It's difficult, emotional work. Being aware of a few self-respecting things you can do for yourself in those moments will keep you from driving yourself back into your grief.

Re-entry

If the healing stage is when the sun occasionally shines through, re-entry is when the sun shines most of the time and only an occasional cloud floats by. Almost without knowing it, you'll be back in the routines of your daily life. But there will still be the occasional moment of remembering, reminders that you have been changed in some very deep ways. Re-entry means you're in the process of going back to your life. When that finally happens for you, there are some important things to know.

- **REMEMBERING**—Memories of big losses never go away; they just get softer and more quiet. Going forward with your life doesn't mean you don't think about your losses anymore, but that you live *with* your memories. As you step back into the world, you'll take your memories and your grief experience with you. They are now part of who you are. They are the stuff that makes you a more mature, sensitive, patient, and supportive person. Growing in this way is one of the gifts in your loss experience.

- **YOU CAN DO IT YOUR WAY**—If you took good care of yourself during your loss, keep it up during your re-entry. It's always a good idea to make sure you are in charge of the pace of things. You'll still need time for reflection, exercise, a reasonable amount of sleep, your faith life, and connections to the important people in your life. If you've been out of the flow of life for a while, it can be easy to get caught up in the swirl and lose yourself on re-entry. If you're feeling overwhelmed, bring yourself back to the schedule that worked for you during The Hard Times. Stay calm and make sure you are in control.

- **TAKE STOCK**—As you get ready to move fully back into your life, you may want to summarize your loss experience. This can be a good time to make a list of your strengths and resources. Make note of the important lessons about life and yourself that you have learned from your experience. After all the thinking, asking "why?" and considering what is really important, you may have some new ideas on how you want to live. You may also have found new support people, a stronger faith life, or a commitment to take better care of yourself physically. Taking a little time to get to know the new "you" can build your confidence and resolve as you re-enter.

I was about six and my dog got hit by a car and we couldn't afford to pay for his injury. I felt very sad about what happened. I learned that if you have a dog near the street unless he is with you, you might want to keep an eye on him.

—Jasmine, Ten

• **MAKE PLANS**—In addition to taking stock you may even want to go to the next step and make some plans based on the lessons you've learned. If your loss resulted from a car accident, you may decide to always wear your seatbelt, to support an organization that promotes safe driving, or to lobby for safer driving laws in your state. You may decide to spend more time with family or with the other people you connected with as a result of your loss. If you lost a dog in an accident with a car, you may decide to keep your new dog on a leash at all times.

Re-entry means going back, but because you have been changed, you may want to live your life differently. It is really up to you. Big losses are often turning points in a person's life. By making some specific plans, you can influence the direction of the turn.

• **BE FORGIVING**—There is an old saying that "Forgiveness relieves one of the burden of revenge." It means that staying angry for a long time can really keep you feeling down and stuck in the past. When you were feeling alone and vulnerable, your feelings were easily hurt. There were probably times in your grief process when someone said the wrong thing, didn't call when they said they would, or embarrassed you in some way. Perhaps you even blame someone else for your loss—"If mom had done... my dog wouldn't have died." You may have gotten so angry that you resolved to get even someday. In your pain and confusion this decision may have made sense.

As you open up to your new life, anger and grudges are just extra baggage. This can be a good time to see if you are still carrying those resentments. Ask yourself again if you want to stay angry or if you are ready to forgive. Then, if you are ready to be forgiving, release your anger. You may write a letter, talk to the person, or simply forgive him or her in your heart. When you're ready, the act of forgiveness will help you make a clean re-entry.

*Today I flow with the river.
I am one with the moon.
I am peaceful and calm.
I forgive myself and everyone
else.*

—Perry Tilleraas

A very important person to forgive is yourself. You can forgive yourself for all the things you didn't do, or say, or become. Maybe you feel bad about how you treated people before or after the loss, how you expressed your anger or frustration, or how you didn't think to say "I love you." In grief, as in life, everyone always does the best they can and still no one manages to do it perfectly. Everyone deserves forgiveness, and that includes you.

THE GIFTS IN LOSS

... we would never learn to be brave and patient if there were only joy in the world.

—Helen Keller

As your understanding and skills for getting through the grief process develop, you get better at coping with all the losses that are such a big part of living. You mature. You accept. In spite of the pain, you grow from the losses in your life. You learn that there are some incredible gifts in even the biggest losses—if you know where to look. Here are just a few.

You Get to Be Human

One of the biggest gifts in loss is learning to be gentle with yourself. Releasing yourself from the need to "keep it all together" and do it "right" as you go through your grief are ways to be self-accepting. When you forgive your past mistakes, you give yourself permission to be human. You learn to love and be gentle with yourself because you are worth it. Accepting yourself as an imperfect person who is deserving of care and love is a gift you can happily take into the rest of your life.

Experiencing Yourself to the Fullest

Getting through a major loss is an enormous personal challenge. You've experienced an incredible array of emotions, gained and lost friendships, and adjusted to major changes in your life. You've been through a lot. In the process, however, you may have discovered you are stronger, more capable, and more resilient than you realized. It's said that we don't really know what we are capable of until we are really tested. A big loss may just help you discover abilities and resources you never realized you had.

Those who do not know how to weep with their whole heart don't know how to laugh either.

—Golda Meir

Emotional Growth

As strange as it sounds, a major gift in a big loss is that we have lots of big feelings. We may experience emotions we didn't know existed and have them with amazing intensity. It may not be pleasant while it's happening, but in the process we develop our emotional equipment. We learn a new language of feelings.

A good example is crying. Some people can go through their life and almost never cry. But after a big loss their tears will be loosened up, crying becomes more acceptable, and they are more likely to cry when they are sad. Being really sad helps us to appreciate feeling good. Because of your experience with deep sadness, your capacity for the positive feelings of love, joy, and gratitude also increases.

The same is true with anger, confusion, hopelessness, and other feelings. The more you experienced them, the more familiar they became. You may now have more ways to express anger or a better understanding of hopelessness and what to do when you feel that way. The gift is that you have more emotional skills to bring to the experience of life.

Considering What's Really Important

Big losses often result in people thinking about what is really important in their lives. Sometimes the things that we worried about the moment before a loss become completely irrelevant the moment after the loss. Your priorities can totally change in response to loss. You might decide to spend more time with loved ones, to travel, to strengthen your faith life, or to stop some self-destructive behavior. You might decide to go to college or learn a trade. Reorganizing how you will live because of what you have been through is a gift that can come from a loss. Often it's an important change in direction for your life that wouldn't have taken place without the loss.

Losses bring me back to reality and make me think about my life and how I want to change it. Even though having a loss is very difficult, it puts everything into a new perspective and gives me a more realistic look on life.

—Mary, Sixteen

When we examine our lives in this way, we are actually building a life: we decide what we want to happen and make a commitment to carry it out. It can be very different from just living a day at a time without much direction. The gift is that as our priorities change, we become more in charge of our lives.

What is obvious to me is that we did not create ourselves... life is something inside of you. You did not create it. Once you understand that, you are in a spiritual realm.

—*Virginia Satir*

A Capacity for Positive Faith

Our existence in an unimaginably huge universe is not something we ever really think about on purpose. It is just too overwhelming. It's not until we run up against a big loss that we stop to ask the big "why" questions. Only then do we realize that we are part of something so much bigger than we can understand. In those moments we can refuse to accept the loss and pound on ourselves or others for answers, or we can simply yield to the power of the universe.

If we choose *not* to accept the loss, we can live for a long time with anger at the universe and all the unanswered questions. In a strange way this is a form of negative faith. It means we have a *belief* that losses are bad things, and that if we keep raging at life, we will eventually get answers we can understand. This is a negative faith because we set ourselves up for long-term frustration and disappointment.

When we are opened up to a spiritual view as the result of our loss, we have another choice. We can choose to believe that there is an order and purpose to our lives, even if we can't understand it all. This belief allows us to accept our losses more easily. We can develop faith, a trust in that order, and believe that things are as they should be. Our faith can

After my loss I forgot about my spiritual life. I regret saying that but it's true. I don't trust anyone or anything. I am not stronger, I am weaker. There is nothing positive left in me. It took it all out of me.

—*Michael, Fifteen*

help us accept that even though we don't like how life is unfolding, things are as they should be. That is a positive faith.

It is pretty hard to come away from a big loss feeling neutral. A positive faith and the comfort it provides is one of the gifts in loss.

You Learn How to Grow

Skills for growing through The Hard Times also happen to be good skills for living. With a big loss you learn that real growth means pushing through hard stuff instead of avoiding it; experiencing some fear, confusion, and uncertainty; being angry, sad, and even hopeless at times. You also learn that it's critical to have support people you can lean on to get through it all. The long process of moving through the different stages of grief teaches you to have patience with yourself when things are difficult. If you are very lucky, you develop a positive faith and acceptance of the things you can't control.

In every instance, I have been led to answers and conclusions which contradict the term loss, because every loss is a gain. If life were a game, each loss would give experience points, which lead to a better game. Never let a loss pull you down. A loss is simply one step back which becomes two steps forward.

—Summer, Seventeen

There is no such thing as a problem without a gift for you in its hands.

—Richard Bach

All of these lessons just happen to be a great tool kit for facing any major challenge in your life. The gift is that you've learned *how to grow.*

Compassion and Forgiveness

If you've learned to be as nice to yourself as you would be to any person who had a similar loss, you've learned compassion. When you can forgive yourself for all those "if onlys," and for not being nice to people in your grief, you have learned forgiveness. Forgiving your-

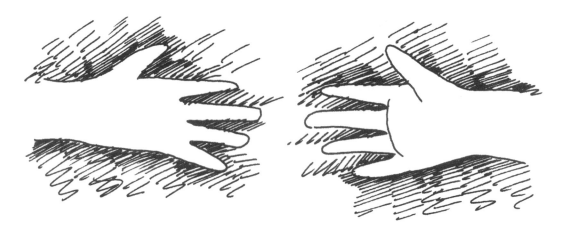

self is a necessary step to being able to forgive others. With compassion and forgiveness in your pocket, you'll be a gentler person and a much better friend to those around you.

Stronger Connection to Others

People drawn together in crisis often form a deep and important connection to each other for the future. It's similar to going through a war, a flood, an earthquake, or a hurricane together. Adversity bonds people together. The people who were there for you when you really needed them earned big points for hanging in there. You know they're reliable and trustworthy and that they'll be there for you in the future. Safety nets of supportive people get stronger with use. One of the gifts from a big loss is that you may have a few more really close friends as you emerge from your grief.

Making the World a Better Place

In the loss pot chapter you learned about some of the ways that the world is a little crazy when it comes to supporting people who are grieving. There are some things you can do to improve the situation however. We learn how to deal with loss from the people around us. That means people watch each other for signals about how to behave. As you go through your losses, you are also teaching someone, somewhere, how to do it.

We know young people tend to look to older kids for signals about how to grow up. Right now, you are a role model, and whether you realize it or not, someone is watching you. By supporting someone who's experiencing a loss or by taking good care of yourself as you grow through your loss, you are giving the world a gift. Because others are watching and learning from your experience, you are a teacher, and you're changing the world in small but important ways. One of the gifts in your loss is the satisfaction that you are making the world a better place.

Helping Others in Grief

Having been through loss and grief, you will have more understanding, patience, and compassion for other people who are suffering. You will be able to understand some of what they are experiencing and what they will have to get through before their lives get back to "normal." Because of your experience, you will be able to support them in ways that are especially helpful. The gift is your increased ability to be there for others whose sadness you understand. The gift is that by helping others in grief, you make the world a little less lonely and frightening.

HOW TO SUPPORT A GRIEVING PERSON

If you have been through The Hard Times, you will know what it is like and naturally have a sense of what helps and what doesn't. You will know that people who are grieving have individual needs, and that the type of support they need changes as they move through the different stages of their loss. You needn't have been through big losses in order to be supportive of a grieving person, but having been there helps. Here are some important ways anyone can be helpful to a person who has had a loss.

STAY CONNECTED: Grieving people have to go through their grief on their own. That's how grieving works. But it can be much less lonely and scary if they know that others care about them and are not too far away if they need a helping hand. Let grieving people know, by your words and actions, that you care, that you will stay by them and be there for them when they need you. Find ways to let them know that they are important to you and that you accept them even (or especially) when they feel the least lovable. When you stay connected, not going away when someone acts weird or moody, you give the grieving person the gift of real friendship.

Right after a big loss, people are often surrounded by supporters. But it's a few weeks later, when the commotion dies down and people go away, that the grieving really settles in. This is a critical time to reach out to help. In the weeks and months of The Hard Times and healing, it is very important to let the grieving person know that you haven't forgotten and that you are still there... for as long as it takes.

> *The greatest gift we can give one another is rapt attention to one another's existence.*
>
> —Sue Atchley Ebaugh

HAVE PATIENCE: As you have learned, people experiencing a loss can be pretty hard to be with at times. Their mood swings, confused thinking, and occasional strange behavior can make them unpleasant to be around. At times they will test your patience, maybe all the time. This behavior is really a signal for you to dig down and gather up all the compassion and patience you can find. Like very sick people, they are just not themselves. They will need your support and they need time to heal—sometimes a long time. Your patience with them is a gift and an expression of true caring.

JUST BE YOU AND BE THERE: It is not your job to fix them, give them great advice, or convince them you know what they are feeling (you really don't). All you have to do is be there and, in your own words, share what's in your heart. It is doing something very important to just be there with them, even not speaking. Someone who is just too exhausted or confused to make conversation often really appreciates silent company.

EXPECT ANGER: People going through a loss have had something taken away. Something they cared about is gone and they should be angry. It's a normal response. Sometimes they are so angry that their anger just jumps out at the wrong times and at the wrong people. Grieving people can be so angry that they will sometimes overreact to the littlest thing. If their anger gets pointed at you, don't be surprised. You may want to consider what they're going through before you respond. Support in this case means not being angry back.

JUST ASK: It hurts to see friends or loved ones struggling with the pain of a loss. We want to make it better or easier for them, but we don't always know how. Mostly we guess at how to be helpful and sometimes do or say the wrong things. We can have good intentions but still give them support that is not helpful or that is even hurtful. One way to be sure you are meeting their needs in the best way is to ask them what kind of support they would like from you. Often they will know and be able to tell you, but at other times they will be such a confused mess that you will be lucky to get a response at all. By asking, regardless of the response, you are letting them know you care and are there for them. That helps a lot.

GROW HUGE EARS: People experiencing a big loss need to talk about it. They need to tell people how strange, sad, confusing, scary, lonely, hopeless, and endless it all feels. They need to say the same things over and over and over again until their wound heals. In fact they need to go on talking about it long after most people have grown tired of listening. If you really want to help people who are grieving, keep asking them how they are doing. Encourage them to talk about their losses by asking questions, staying interested, and listening as long as you can. Your having big ears and a willingness to use them is very helpful to a grieving person.

REMEMBER ANNIVERSARIES: The passage of time changes for a person experiencing a major loss. Often it moves very, very slowly and just getting through a week can seem like forever. Remembering anniversaries like a week, month, or even a year since the loss with a call, a note, or a card helps in a number of ways. It reminds them that time *is* passing and they *are* getting through The Hard Times. Reminders also let them know that you care enough to pay attention to their life and that you are interested in how they are doing.

HELP THEM SEE THE UPSIDE: At some point a ways down the road from a big loss, people will be ready to consider again how they and the world are wonderful. But in the early days and months of a loss, it's hard to let it in. Trying to force someone to consider the upside too soon is not helpful at all. When they appear to be putting themselves back together, your help in remembering the good stuff of life and how they are amazing, awesome, playful, cool, competent, and lovable can be very helpful.

EXPLORING YOUR LOSS POT

As your skills for growing through the natural and difficult losses of life increase, you will be stuffing less and less sadness into your loss pot. But that still leaves all those old losses in the pot. Because all those old losses get mixed up into a big sad stew, it's easy to confuse feelings about new losses with all the old stuff. Plus it takes a lot of energy to carry all that heaviness around. If you want to be really well prepared to cope with future losses, you may want to lighten your load. The only way to do that is to reach into the pot and re-examine the old losses. A good place to begin is to measure the fullness of your loss pot.

Loss pots fill up gradually as we stuff our hurts into them over the years. As a result, we can gradually become more serious and depressed without realizing it. The effects accumulate so slowly that you can change dramatically and not even be aware you're different. For that reason, it's a good idea to check yourself out every once in a while to see if it's time to clean out the pot.

People who have a lot of stuff in their loss pot often share the traits listed below. Keep in mind that people can have these symptoms for reasons other than a full loss pot. But whatever the cause, if you can answer yes to more than a couple of the following questions, you may want to reach out for some objectivity and support.

Measuring Your Loss Pot

Do my feelings get really stirred up on the anniversary day of a big loss?

Am I constantly aware of the loss, even if it happened years ago?

Am I using the loss to be treated "special" long after the loss event?

Am I still angry and bitter at people, the universe, life, fate... years later because of my loss?

Do I have trouble being playful or having fun? Is it hard to just feel happy and to laugh?

Do certain songs, movies, places, smells, or holidays make me *really* sad and stir up uncomfortable feelings?

Do I need to avoid reminders of the loss in order to keep myself together?

Do I hang out with people who are angry and serious?

Is hurting others an acceptable behavior among my friends?

Do I often feel hopeless, not caring about my grades, appearance, health, or anything?

Would other people say I am serious/sad/depressed?

If I open up to the memory of old losses, do I feel the rumblings of big feelings?

Do I think other people are weak because they have such strong feelings about loss?

Would others say I am hard to get to know? Do I wear a shell to protect myself from others and the world?

Do I have problems showing my feelings to other people?

Am I highly emotional? Can just about anything bring me to tears?

Do I get uncomfortable being with people who are going through The Hard Times and having big feelings?

Lots of "yeses" to these questions is an indication that you may have a full loss pot. Full loss pots don't empty out on their own. You either do the work necessary to empty the old losses or drag your loss pot through life. Those are your options.

Just like you've learned about the skills for dealing with a loss, you can use another set of skills for working through old, stuffed losses. When you get better at not stuffing new losses and learn the skills of working through old losses, you'll be able to keep your loss pot pretty empty. That means you will be a lighter, happier person and will be better equipped to cope with the challenges of living.

Working Through Old Losses

If you feel that now is a good time in your life to look into your loss pot and begin to sort out the past, there are some skills you can learn.

Get a Guide

Exploring old losses does mean heading back into complicated emotional territory. Because you are choosing to go there, you won't be as vulnerable as you were when the original losses occurred, but it can still be a difficult experience. You'll want an experienced guide who knows the territory and who has the ability to stick with you through the emotional challenges you'll encounter. The guide can help you stay on track. A professional counselor, minister, or loss support group can provide the experienced help you need. They can help you take care of yourself along the way.

The only risks have to do with getting lost in places like old hurt, anger, and resentment. That's why guides and support are so important. They can keep you on track, keep you from getting stuck, keep you from running away and restuffing the feelings back in the pot. Your guides and support people are your safety net.

Make a Commitment

Working through your old losses is a significant personal challenge. It's like deciding to quit smoking, getting more exercise, doing your homework, being on time for meetings, or carrying out any other self-improvement activity. You have to make a commitment to yourself to do whatever it takes to reach your goal, even when the going gets tough, because you are worth it.

Telling a few trusted friends what you're up to will enhance your level of commitment. When you make yourself accountable to others and ask for their support, the challenges seem less frightening.

> ## We are all in this alone... together.
>
> —*Alcoholics Anonymous saying*

Unpack the Memories

Working through the past is like unpacking a suitcase full of old things. You find the suitcase, open it up, and take out the stuff inside one item at a time. With each item, you pause to re-experience the memories and feelings the article stirs up. Some of the memories will be stronger than others and have lots of details. Other items will draw a com-

plete blank. Some of the old memories will have lots of feelings attached and some will have no effect on you at all. Some memories will be of very happy moments you had forgotten about completely. But you'll also find old wounds, hurts, anger, and resentments.

Once you get started, you'll probably find the old memories naturally coming to you. Old hurts "want" to be healed. But if you draw a blank you can start by looking at the life line of loss events you created on page 10. Pick one of those early losses and focus on it.

Write about the loss in your journal, find objects that relate to that period in your life, look at old photos of yourself at that age, and talk to your relatives to learn more about what your life was like around the time of the loss. Or you can just lie down, close your eyes, and invite the memories to come.

When old feelings and memories do start to show up, share them with your guide or others you trust. Tell them what your experience of the loss was like... *have* the feelings that have been cooking in the loss pot all these years.

> ## We are healed of a suffering only by experiencing it to the full.
>
> —Marcel Proust

Whatever method you use to empty your loss pot, it is better than never lifting the lid. By going through this process you re-experience the loss events and feelings. You give yourself the chance to grow through the old hurts in the present, when you're ready and better able to cope than you were the day you stuffed them away. On the other hand, if you think that having the feelings associated with loss and grief is a bad thing, you're probably not ready to do this work.

Growing Through the Past

Growing through the past should be a process of discovery. You will be surprised as forgotten memories and feelings pop up and ask to be experienced again. Experiencing old losses in the present, sorting through the old mental, physical, emotional, or spiritual wounds and allowing them to heal is the "work" of emptying your loss pot.

With this work comes a new understanding of the loss, changes in destructive thinking, and willingness to forgive. You'll find gifts in the old losses. You may discover new strengths, renewed relationships, and positive feelings about yourself, or have new ideas about what you want to do with your life. Acceptance of our losses, as opposed to denying and stuffing our feelings, liberates us to grow. Our load gets lighter and a new person almost always results.

WHAT KIDS HAVE LEARNED ABOUT LOSS AND GRIEF

It hurts but there are good people who will help you through it. Be strong, but talk to someone. You may always hurt some from it, but you can learn to deal with loss and accept it.

—Holly, Seventeen

Talk about your loss, think before you react, don't rely on chemicals.

—Eric, Fifteen

When my grandmother Marie died I was about nine years old. She died of pneumonia because she was old and she couldn't handle it. I felt horrible because we were really close. One lesson I learned is that everyone dies at some time and that it was her turn to go.

—Heather, Twelve

I learned nothing in this world is permanent.

—Mike, Sixteen

Don't try to analyze the loss. Take it in, mourn for the loss, however long it takes, process it with others, and then let it go. Keeping a hold of the anger will only make you bitter and create future problems.

—Vanessa, Eighteen

The only way to get over it is to deal with it.

—Jenny, Fifteen

*I learned to look at the bright side and not always the negative.
Tomorrow's another day, live to the extreme, you are young, live your life,
don't make a complete mess out of a simply bad situation.*

—Shawnee, Seventeen

My respect for others and myself helped me get through bad times.

—Neil, Sixteen

*When I was eight, my grandma died. I learned you have to accept things for what they
are, and live your life one day at a time. If you spend too much time thinking
about the future and too much time in the past, it is like having one foot in the future
and one in the past and today means nothing. You'll waste your life.*

—Steven, Nineteen

*I was so close to losing my life because of cancer and I was not going to let go
and give up because of one setback. My spirituality and my love of music
helped me the most.*

—Jessica, Seventeen

I just told myself that I could do it.

—Trista, Fifteen

*There really aren't strengths involved, you just do it. You learn to face things
and relate to many different people. It is part of growing up.*

—Drew, Fourteen

*Just the simple fact that I believe in God and eternal life lets me believe that those
who have gone before me are safe, happy, and at peace.*

—Jessica, Seventeen

My loss helped me get more in touch with my feelings.

—Steven, Nineteen

When my parents got divorced I had to make the decision of which one to live with. I was really afraid because I didn't want to hurt either of them. I finally realized that I couldn't base my decision on their needs; I had to think about myself and what I wanted. This big life lesson, stick up for yourself, is really important to me now.

—Lindsay, Fifteen

Now I know what real loss is like. I know what it means to have someone die.

—Justin, Sixteen

My attitude is better, I accept being wrong, have an open mind, I'm more positive, and I am not afraid of asking for help.

—Michele, Fourteen

I think that my grandmas dying helped me realize that death isn't always something to fear.

—Katie, Fifteen

I learned people really care about me.

—John, Seventeen

Life is short, live for today.

—Steven, Nineteen

That you shouldn't dread on it because then it only gets worse.

—Justin, Sixteen

Not to take anything for granted because one minute you're here and the next you could be gone.

—Sarah, Sixteen

If life sucks now maybe it will get better later.

—Neil, Sixteen

I learned that I could really help myself out of it if I tried and worked on it. I also learned how to take my problems out in a better way.

—Trista, Fifteen

That big losses will happen, and you will just have to learn to roll with it.
—Tim, Sixteen

There is beauty in everything… and not many things,
like your worst fears will kill you.
—Katie, Sixteen

GOING FOR IT

Losses are a big part of life. We will all experience many thousands of losses as we grow older. Like other kinds of experience, losses can be about developing, struggling, learning, accepting, discovering ourselves, understanding life, appreciating our connections to others, and finding our place in the natural order of things.

In a perfect world, you would understand your loss, take great care of yourself as you go through the process of grief, experience your feelings fully, surround yourself with supportive and caring people, never lose hope, find many of the gifts that can come out of your grief experience, and grow into a stronger person as a result.

Experience is not what happens to you, it is what you do with what happens to you.

—Aldous Huxley

But we don't live in a perfect world. By reading this book you have increased your understanding of loss and grief. You are now aware of better choices to make when facing losses. You can take better care of yourself and be more supportive to others in grief. You are also better prepared to face life. People who understand loss and grief are better able to face life boldly. They can take the necessary risks in life, knowing that when losses occur, they can survive, get through, and very likely grow as a result.

I have learned that life is too precious to waste. I don't take unnecessary risks, but I also don't sit on my butt all day, afraid to venture outside my room. Life is fun and I'm not holding back!

—Jessica, Seventeen

Many people gave of themselves to put this book in your hands in this moment. We all hope that what you have learned will help ease your suffering, help you heal cleanly, and help you become a stronger and more resilient young person. We hope that you'll have less fear, more courage, and more self-confidence and that you'll live your life more boldly and not hold back.

Remember, you are a miracle of the universe, take good care of yourself and go for it.

—Earl, Fifty-one

INDEX

Earl Hipp is very interested in your comments on this book. What parts of the book helped you, what you liked best, or what other topics you would like to see in future editions. He is interested in hearing about your experiences with loss and grief and the lessons you have learned. Earl is also available to speak to groups.

You can contact Earl by writing him at

Earl Hipp
Human Resource Development, Inc.
2938 Monterey Ave.
Minneapolis, MN 55416

Other books by Earl Hipp include *Feed Your Head: Some Excellent Stuff on Being Yourself*; *Fighting Invisible Tigers: A Stress Management Guide for Teens*; and *The Caring Circle: A Facilitator's Guide to Support Groups*. You can order these books by calling Hazelden at: **1-800-328-0098**.

About Hazelden Publishing

As part of the Hazelden Betty Ford Foundation, Hazelden Publishing offers both cutting-edge educational resources and inspirational books. Our print and digital works help guide individuals in treatment and recovery, and their loved ones. Professionals who work to prevent and treat addiction also turn to Hazelden Publishing for evidence-based curricula, digital content solutions, and videos for use in schools, treatment programs, correctional programs, and electronic health records systems. We also offer training for implementation of our curricula.

Through published and digital works, Hazelden Publishing extends the reach of healing and hope to individuals, families, and communities affected by addiction and related issues.

For more information about Hazelden publications,
please call **800-328-9000**
or visit us online at **hazelden.org/bookstore**.

Another book by Earl Hipp and L. K. Hanson…

Feed Your Head
Some Excellent Stuff on Being Yourself
written by Earl Hipp, illustrated by L. K. Hanson

Author Earl Hipp helps young people make their way through the daily maze of questions, worries, ups and downs, problems, and puzzles. With a light touch—and lots of humor—this survival guide for ages 11 to 17 creates a map for handling crises, emotions, and responsibilities. Topics focus on the "ABCs" of self-help, peer pressure and the need to belong, the warning signs of trouble, the definition of friendship, and more. 138 pp.

Order No. 5034